CW01512055

Wonders of the Mediterranean: Empires Along the Sea

Anam Rasheed

Published by Anam Rasheed, 2024.

While every precaution has been taken in the preparation of this book, the publisher assumes no responsibility for errors or omissions, or for damages resulting from the use of the information contained herein.

WONDERS OF THE MEDITERRANEAN: EMPIRES ALONG THE SEA

First edition. November 8, 2024.

Copyright © 2024 Anam Rasheed.

ISBN: 979-8227425492

Written by Anam Rasheed.

Table of Contents

Prologue

Imagine standing on the shores of the Mediterranean Sea, feeling the warm sun on your skin and listening to the waves gently crashing at your feet. For thousands of years, people have gathered along these shores, gazing out across the water toward distant lands and new adventures. The Mediterranean Sea has been a place of discovery, a gateway for explorers, a treasure trove for traders, and a battlefield for empires. From the powerful ships of ancient Greece to the bustling markets of Carthage, this sea has shaped the lives of countless civilizations, weaving together their stories like a giant, shimmering tapestry.

In this book, we'll journey back through time to meet some of the most daring, inventive, and determined people who ever lived. You'll read about kings and queens, explorers and inventors, warriors and sailors. They built empires, sailed to unknown places, traded exotic goods, and fought for control of these sparkling blue waters. From the legendary city of Troy to the towering pyramids of Egypt, each chapter reveals a new wonder and a new story from the Mediterranean world.

As we travel across centuries and cultures, you'll discover how this sea became a powerful force in history—helping to spread ideas, create art, and even inspire myths and legends. So, get ready to set sail on a thrilling adventure through time and place. The Mediterranean has many secrets, and they're waiting for you to dive in and explore!

Chapter 1: The Birth of the Mediterranean Sea

Millions of years ago, the land and seas on Earth looked very different from how they do now. The Mediterranean Sea, one of the world's most famous bodies of water, didn't even exist back then. Instead, there were giant landmasses and oceans shifting around due to movements deep below the Earth's surface. This shifting of huge land plates is known as "plate tectonics." Over time, these plates bumped into each other, pulled apart, or slid past one another, which changed the shapes of continents and oceans. At the time, there was a massive ancient ocean called the Tethys Sea where the Mediterranean is today. Slowly, the movements of these plates would give birth to the Mediterranean Sea we know now.

About 50 million years ago, the African plate, carrying the land we now call Africa, began to move northward, colliding with the Eurasian plate, which held parts of Europe and Asia. As these two massive plates pushed against each other, they created pressure that forced some land to rise up, forming the earliest versions of mountain ranges like the Alps and the Pyrenees. As land shifted and lifted, parts of the Tethys Sea were squeezed and trapped. This gradual closing of the Tethys Sea over millions of years began forming smaller bodies of water, which would eventually include the Mediterranean Sea.

One of the most astonishing events in the Mediterranean's history occurred around six million years ago, during a time called the "Messinian Salinity Crisis." In this period, the connection between the Atlantic Ocean and the Mediterranean was cut off, possibly because land rose and blocked the narrow strait that linked them. This separation caused the Mediterranean to nearly dry up, turning much of it into a vast, salty desert. Imagine a place where today's beautiful blue sea lies – now a dry basin with layers of salt and minerals baking under the sun. Rivers and streams from nearby lands brought a little water into the basin, but it wasn't enough to fill the whole area. Over time, thick layers of salt and minerals built up on the seabed, some of which are still there deep below the current sea floor. This dry, salty period went on for hundreds of thousands of years.

Then, about five million years ago, an enormous event took place. The barrier that had cut off the Mediterranean from the Atlantic finally broke down, possibly due to the movement of tectonic plates or rising sea levels. The Atlantic Ocean rushed into the Mediterranean Basin through the Strait of Gibraltar in a massive flood that might have taken only a few months or even weeks. Some scientists believe the water poured in with incredible force, refilling the dry basin and transforming it back into a sea in a very short time. Imagine waterfalls the size of mountains crashing down as the ocean returned to fill the empty space! This event, often called the "Zanclean Flood," marks the beginning of the Mediterranean as a large, connected sea once more.

Since then, the Mediterranean Sea has continued to change, though more slowly. Rivers from surrounding lands carried sediments like sand, mud, and rocks into the sea, which settled on the seabed over time. Volcanoes also played a part, with underwater eruptions and volcanic islands like Sicily and Santorini forming from the activity below the sea. The Mediterranean region is still geologically active today, with earthquakes and occasional volcanic eruptions reminding us of the powerful forces that shaped it.

Because of its warm climate, deep blue waters, and location between three continents—Europe, Africa, and Asia—the Mediterranean became an attractive place for people to settle. Its shores were ideal for fishing, farming, and trade, with calm bays and natural harbors perfect for boats. In ancient times, civilizations grew along its coastlines, such as the Egyptians, Greeks, Phoenicians, and Romans, who built bustling cities and used the Mediterranean as a highway for exploration, trade, and war. The sea's long history and its unique position made it one of the most influential regions in human history, linking distant lands and cultures.

Today, the Mediterranean Sea is still one of the world's busiest waterways, carrying ships that trade goods and transport people between Europe, Africa, and Asia. Scientists continue to study the sea's past to understand how it formed and changed over millions of years, looking at clues from the rocks, fossils, and seabed. Each discovery tells us a bit more about how powerful natural forces created this special sea.

Chapter 2: Ancient Greece and the Heroes of the Waves

Ancient Greece was a land of bustling city-states, incredible stories, and some of the world's most famous thinkers, warriors, and adventurers. These city-states, like Athens, Sparta, and Corinth, were scattered across the Greek mainland, islands, and along the coast of the Mediterranean Sea. But to the Greeks, the Mediterranean wasn't just a body of water—it was a world of possibilities. This sea allowed them to explore, trade, and conquer new lands, and it became the stage for tales of heroism and adventure. For ancient Greeks, who lived in small, often isolated communities surrounded by mountains or coastlines, the sea was the way to reach distant lands. It became their pathway to the world beyond, a place where legends and real-life heroes mixed, creating stories that are still told today.

The Greeks were expert sailors and shipbuilders, and the sea was central to their lives. They built sturdy ships with large sails and rows of oars so that they could travel across the waves. The most famous of these vessels was the trireme, a powerful warship with three rows of oars on each side, each oar operated by a strong and dedicated rower. These ships could move incredibly fast, thanks to the teamwork of the rowers and the guidance of skilled captains. Triremes allowed the Greeks to defend their cities, expand their territories, and trade goods like olive oil, wine, and pottery across the Mediterranean and beyond.

The Greeks didn't just use the sea for trade and war; it was also the source of countless myths and legends. Greek mythology is filled with tales of gods, monsters, and brave heroes who traveled across the Mediterranean. Perhaps the most famous of these sea heroes was Odysseus, the clever king of Ithaca. After fighting in the Trojan War, Odysseus set sail for home, but his journey was anything but easy. During his long voyage, he encountered giant cyclopes, dangerous sirens who tried to lure his crew into traps with their enchanting songs, and the powerful sea god Poseidon, who held a grudge against him. Through his courage, wit, and determination, Odysseus managed to overcome these dangers and return to Ithaca, but only after many years. His story, known as "The Odyssey," became one of the most famous adventure tales ever told, inspiring people across generations with its lessons of bravery and perseverance.

Another famous hero connected to the sea was Jason, leader of the Argonauts. Jason's quest was to find the Golden Fleece, a magical object guarded by a fearsome dragon far from Greece. To achieve this, he gathered a team of the bravest and strongest men in Greece, including Heracles, the strongest man alive, and Orpheus, a musician whose songs could charm even the most fearsome creatures. Together, they set sail on the Argo, a legendary ship, and faced numerous challenges along the way. They had to navigate through narrow straits guarded by deadly sea monsters, fight off magical creatures, and solve tricky puzzles. Jason's adventure, known as "The Quest for the Golden Fleece," became a story of teamwork and bravery that showed the Greeks' love for tales of the sea.

The Greek love for the sea was also reflected in their worship of gods and goddesses. Poseidon, the god of the sea, was one of the most powerful deities in the Greek pantheon. Greeks believed that he could control storms, create earthquakes, and calm the waves, so they often prayed and offered sacrifices to him before setting sail. Sailors and fishermen looked to Poseidon for protection and guidance, hoping he would grant them safe journeys. Temples were built in his honor along the coasts, and rituals were held to keep him pleased, as upsetting Poseidon could lead to dangerous waters and fierce storms. Other sea-related deities included Amphitrite, Poseidon's queen, and the Nereids, sea nymphs who were said to help sailors in times of trouble.

As the Greeks traveled across the Mediterranean, they established colonies and trading posts in faraway lands. Places like Sicily, southern

Italy, and parts of North Africa became home to Greek settlers who brought with them their language, customs, and culture. These colonies grew into vibrant cities that connected the Greeks with people from other cultures, like the Phoenicians and Egyptians. This contact helped spread Greek ideas about democracy, philosophy, and art, making the Mediterranean a melting pot of different cultures and beliefs. The Greeks were curious about the world and wanted to learn from others, and the sea allowed them to do that.

Greek sailors and merchants weren't just interested in material goods; they also brought back knowledge and ideas. They learned about astronomy from the Egyptians, picked up new building techniques from the Phoenicians, and adopted coinage systems that made trade easier. The sea was a pathway not only for goods like silver, spices, and glass but also for thoughts and innovations. This exchange of knowledge helped the Greeks build cities, create art, and understand the world in ways that hadn't been done before. The Mediterranean was like a classroom for the Greeks, offering lessons with each journey.

In their theaters, Greeks would tell these sea tales through plays, and poets like Homer would recount the great deeds of heroes through epic poems. The sea adventures of figures like Odysseus and Jason weren't just for entertainment; they taught important values like courage, loyalty, and cleverness. Greek children grew up hearing these stories, imagining themselves as brave adventurers crossing the Mediterranean, facing unknown dangers, and returning home victorious. These stories became part of Greek culture, passed down through generations and shaping how the Greeks viewed themselves as brave, curious people ready to explore the world.

Ancient Greece's connection to the Mediterranean Sea influenced its entire civilization. The sea gave the Greeks food from fishing, wealth from trading, and inspiration for myths and stories. The heroes of the waves, both real and legendary, helped shape a culture that admired courage, exploration, and adventure. Through their tales, they left behind a legacy that has endured for thousands of years. Today, we still remember these heroes, their incredible journeys, and the sea that connected them to the world. The Mediterranean was more than just a sea to the Greeks; it was a place of magic, mystery, and endless adventure.

Chapter 3: Rome's Mighty Empire and Its Coastal Reach

Rome began as a small city along the Tiber River in Italy, but over the centuries, it grew into one of the largest empires the world had ever seen. With powerful armies, brilliant strategies, and strong leaders, Rome expanded its borders far beyond Italy, conquering lands across Europe, North Africa, and parts of Asia. This vast empire stretched from the chilly coasts of Britain to the hot sands of Egypt and from Spain's western shores to the deserts of the Middle East. At the center of it all was the Mediterranean Sea, which the Romans called "Mare Nostrum," or "Our Sea." They saw the Mediterranean as the heart of their empire, linking distant provinces and connecting people, goods, and ideas across vast distances.

The Romans were skilled builders and planners, and their success in controlling such a large empire depended greatly on the sea. The Mediterranean allowed Roman ships to travel quickly between regions, making it easier to move soldiers, supplies, and trade goods. Rome's naval power grew strong enough to keep the sea lanes safe from pirates and hostile forces, allowing traders to transport valuable items like grain from Egypt, olive oil from Spain, and spices from the East. To maintain control, the Romans built a series of ports and harbors along the coasts of their empire, including major ports in places like Ostia in Italy, Alexandria in Egypt, and Carthage in North Africa. These ports became bustling centers of trade and commerce, where merchants from different cultures met and exchanged goods and stories.

One of Rome's greatest strengths was its navy, which patrolled the Mediterranean to keep it safe for Roman interests. In the early days, Rome didn't have a navy and struggled against enemies like Carthage, a powerful city in North Africa with its own mighty fleet. But during the Punic Wars, a series of conflicts between Rome and Carthage, the

Romans built a powerful navy from scratch, learning quickly how to fight on the sea. They even invented a clever device called the "corvus," a long plank with a metal spike that allowed Roman soldiers to board enemy ships. With this tool and their determined soldiers, Rome eventually defeated Carthage and took control of its territories. This victory was a major turning point, as it gave Rome control over much of the western Mediterranean and showed the world that they were a force to be reckoned with on both land and sea.

With Carthage defeated, Rome expanded its reach, conquering new lands along the Mediterranean coast. The Romans were especially interested in Egypt, which was one of the most fertile regions in the ancient world. The Nile River's rich soil allowed Egyptian farmers to grow vast amounts of grain, which was essential for feeding Rome's growing population. Egypt eventually became a Roman province, and grain shipments from Alexandria became vital for the empire. Special ships called grain carriers sailed from Egypt to Rome, bringing enough food to feed the city's thousands of citizens. The Mediterranean Sea made it possible for this food to be transported quickly and efficiently, preventing famines and keeping Rome strong.

Rome's coastal reach wasn't just about trade and resources; it also allowed them to spread their culture and influence. As they conquered new lands, the Romans built cities that looked and functioned much like Rome itself. These cities had grand temples, theaters, baths, and arenas where people could gather, worship, and be entertained. Places like Caesarea in Israel, Leptis Magna in North Africa, and Tarragona in Spain became important Roman cities, showcasing Roman architecture, law, and culture. The Romans built impressive aqueducts to bring fresh water to their cities, paved roads that connected distant regions, and massive amphitheaters where citizens could watch gladiators and wild animals in fierce battles. These structures weren't just for show—they symbolized Roman power and civilization, reminding people of the might of the Roman Empire.

The sea also allowed Roman soldiers, known as legionaries, to travel quickly to troubled areas. When rebellions broke out in far-off provinces, or when foreign invaders threatened Roman lands, the legions could board ships and sail across the Mediterranean to defend the empire. These disciplined, well-trained soldiers became famous for their courage and skill, and their presence along the coasts ensured that the empire remained secure. The Roman army's ability to control both land and sea made it incredibly difficult for enemies to challenge them. Even in rough waters or stormy weather, the Romans found ways to keep their ships moving, thanks to their determination and advanced sailing techniques.

Roman leaders understood that controlling the Mediterranean gave them a strategic advantage, so they focused on building and maintaining strong defenses along the coasts. They established forts and watchtowers on distant shores to keep an eye out for potential threats and built massive walls around their most important cities. For example, in Constantinople, the Romans constructed a series of walls that protected the city from invasions by sea. These fortifications allowed Rome to feel secure, knowing that their enemies would struggle to penetrate the empire's defenses.

Beyond soldiers and buildings, the Mediterranean Sea became a place where different cultures met and mixed under Roman rule. People from various parts of the empire traveled by sea to Rome's heart, bringing their traditions, languages, and ideas with them. Roman cities became melting pots where Egyptians, Greeks, Gauls, Syrians, and others lived side by side, contributing to a rich and diverse culture. Greek philosophy, Egyptian art, and Eastern spices all became part of Roman life, blending together to create a unique culture that was both Roman and international. The Mediterranean Sea, with its network of ports and ships, made this exchange of ideas possible, enriching the empire and making it one of the most cosmopolitan societies of its time.

Rome's coastal reach allowed it to control valuable resources from across the empire. The Spanish coast provided silver, Africa yielded olives and wild animals for the games, and the Levant region offered valuable timber and purple dye. The Romans developed efficient systems to extract these resources, making Rome wealthy and powerful. Their system of trade and transport was so well-organized that goods could move across the empire faster than ever before, allowing the empire to thrive and grow for centuries.

In the end, Rome's mastery of the Mediterranean Sea played a huge role in its rise as a superpower. The empire's leaders, soldiers, merchants, and citizens all relied on the Mediterranean for survival and success. When the empire eventually began to decline, invaders from outside disrupted these sea routes, attacking Roman ships and ports. As Rome lost control of the Mediterranean, its ability to rule such a vast territory weakened, leading to its eventual fall. But during its height, the Roman Empire's coastal reach was unmatched, and the Mediterranean was truly their "Mare Nostrum," a symbol of their power, unity, and connection across the ancient world.

Chapter 4: The Phoenician Sailors and the Secrets of Trade

The Phoenicians were an extraordinary group of people who lived along the eastern coast of the Mediterranean Sea, in what is now Lebanon, Syria, and parts of northern Israel. Unlike the Greeks and Romans, the Phoenicians weren't known for building empires or conquering lands. Instead, they were skilled sailors, traders, and navigators, known for their adventurous spirit and keen sense for business. The Mediterranean Sea was like a vast highway for them, and they were masters at traveling across it. The Phoenicians used the sea to establish trade networks that spanned from the coasts of North Africa to distant parts of Europe, creating one of the ancient world's first international trading systems.

The Phoenicians built sturdy, swift ships that allowed them to sail long distances, carrying goods from one place to another. They constructed their vessels from cedarwood, which was strong and resistant to decay, making their ships durable enough to withstand long journeys and challenging sea conditions. These ships were designed with a curved hull that allowed them to cut smoothly through the water, and they were often equipped with a single large sail to harness the wind. Phoenician ships also had rows of oarsmen who could propel the vessel forward even when there was no wind, making the ships fast and reliable. Thanks to their innovative shipbuilding techniques, the Phoenicians could travel farther and faster than many of their neighbors, establishing a reputation as the Mediterranean's top traders.

Trade was the lifeblood of the Phoenician people, and they were known for their ability to find valuable goods that other cultures wanted. They were expert merchants, dealing in a variety of items that were rare or highly desired across the Mediterranean. One of their most famous products was purple dye, which they made from a type of sea snail called the murex. This dye was incredibly difficult to produce, requiring thousands of snails to make even a small amount, so it became very expensive. Purple cloth, dyed with this rich color, became a symbol of wealth and royalty, and rulers across the ancient world were eager to buy it. This valuable purple dye earned the Phoenicians a great deal of wealth and even led to them being nicknamed the "purple people."

In addition to purple dye, the Phoenicians traded goods like glass, fine pottery, cedarwood, and metalwork. They were some of the first people to produce transparent glass, which was highly prized by the Egyptians and other cultures. The glass was often shaped into small beads, bowls, and decorative items, making it a popular trade item. Cedarwood, from the forests of Lebanon, was another important product, as it was strong and resistant to pests, making it perfect for building ships, temples, and palaces. The Egyptians and other cultures eagerly bought this wood, as it was far better than what was available in their own lands. The Phoenicians even traded luxury goods like ivory carvings and jewelry, which they obtained from Africa and Asia, making their trade routes and offerings incredibly diverse.

The Phoenicians didn't just trade goods; they also spread ideas, cultures, and knowledge. One of their greatest contributions to history was the development of the alphabet, which made writing simpler and more accessible. Unlike complex writing systems such as Egyptian hieroglyphs, the Phoenician alphabet used symbols to represent sounds, making it much easier to learn and use. This alphabet was so practical that it spread across the Mediterranean, influencing the Greek alphabet and, eventually, the writing systems used in Europe today. As Phoenician traders traveled from port to port, they brought this alphabet with them, teaching it to others and changing how people communicated across vast distances.

The Phoenicians were some of the first people to establish colonies, which were settlements in foreign lands that served as bases for their trade activities. As they sailed across the Mediterranean, they set up colonies in key locations, where they could store goods, repair their ships, and continue their trading missions. Some of these colonies grew into thriving cities, like Carthage in North Africa, which eventually became a powerful city-state in its own right. Carthage was strategically located, allowing the Phoenicians to control trade routes that passed through the western Mediterranean. This city became one of the most important and wealthiest colonies in the Phoenician network, demonstrating the effectiveness of their trading empire.

To navigate such long distances, the Phoenicians developed advanced knowledge of the sea and stars. They studied the patterns of the stars to help guide their way, even when they were far from land. At night, they used the North Star to help keep their ships on course, and during the day, they watched for land features and landmarks. The Phoenicians also understood the seasonal changes in wind patterns and ocean currents, which allowed them to plan their voyages more effectively. They were careful observers of the natural world, learning from their journeys and passing this knowledge down from one generation to the next.

The Phoenicians faced many dangers on the open sea, including storms, pirates, and unfriendly foreign powers. However, they developed a strong sense of resilience and bravery, navigating these risks to protect their valuable cargo. They often traveled in convoys, or groups of ships, to protect themselves from attacks, and they built strongholds and fortified ports to keep their colonies safe. The Phoenicians were not warriors, but they knew how to defend themselves when necessary, and they earned respect for their courage and resourcefulness.

As their trade networks expanded, the Phoenicians became very wealthy, and their cities flourished. In cities like Tyre, Sidon, and Byblos, skilled artisans created beautiful works of art, jewelry, and pottery, which were sold across the Mediterranean. Their temples and palaces were decorated with intricate carvings and bright colors, showcasing the wealth and skill of the Phoenician people. The Phoenicians celebrated their prosperity with festivals and rituals that honored their gods, such as Baal, the god of fertility, and Astarte, the goddess of love and war. These religious traditions traveled with them to other lands, influencing the cultures they encountered.

The Phoenician way of life was deeply connected to the sea, and their legacy lives on in the coastal towns and cities they built. Their skill as sailors, their ability to connect distant lands, and their love of exploration made them legendary figures in ancient history. Even after their cities were eventually conquered by larger empires, like the Assyrians, Babylonians, and Persians, the influence of the Phoenicians remained. Their alphabet continued to be used, their colonies carried on, and their contributions to trade, art, and culture became an enduring part of the Mediterranean world.

Through their adventurous spirit, the Phoenicians created connections that linked cultures and helped build a network of shared knowledge, goods, and ideas. They weren't just merchants; they were pioneers, creating one of the ancient world's most sophisticated and far-reaching trade networks. The Phoenicians took secrets of the sea and made them their own, becoming legendary sailors and traders whose impact can still be felt today. Their story reminds us of the power of curiosity, innovation, and resilience, and the incredible things that can happen when people set sail to explore the unknown.

Chapter 5: Egypt's Pharaohs and the Nile to the Mediterranean

The ancient Egyptians lived in a remarkable land shaped by the Nile River, which flowed from deep in Africa, through deserts and fertile plains, and finally into the Mediterranean Sea. This river was the lifeblood of Egypt, providing water, food, and a way to travel and trade. The Egyptian civilization flourished along the Nile for thousands of years, and the pharaohs, Egypt's powerful kings, ruled over this land with strength and wisdom. The Nile was so essential to Egypt's existence that the Egyptians called it a gift from the gods, and they believed that it connected them to the rest of the world through its journey to the Mediterranean.

The Nile was the longest river in the world, and its annual flooding was essential for Egyptian farming. Each year, the river overflowed its banks, leaving behind a thick layer of rich, black silt. This silt made the soil incredibly fertile, perfect for growing crops like wheat, barley, and flax, which the Egyptians used to make linen. Because of the Nile's yearly floods, the Egyptians could farm and harvest large amounts of food, which allowed them to develop a strong society. Without the Nile, Egypt might have been just another dry desert, but instead, it became one of the ancient world's greatest civilizations.

The pharaohs ruled over this civilization and were seen as both powerful kings and divine figures. The Egyptians believed their pharaohs were chosen by the gods and that they themselves were living gods on Earth. Pharaohs like Ramses II, Tutankhamun, and Cleopatra left lasting legacies, not only in Egypt but also in the lands they conquered or allied with. Many of these rulers wanted Egypt to be known far beyond its borders, and they worked to extend Egypt's reach toward the Mediterranean, where they could trade and communicate with other civilizations like the Greeks, Phoenicians, and Romans.

Egypt's connection to the Mediterranean allowed it to become a significant power in the ancient world, influencing art, religion, and trade across the region.

The Nile also made it possible for the Egyptians to build incredible structures, like the Great Pyramids of Giza, the Sphinx, and massive temples dedicated to gods like Amun-Ra, Osiris, and Isis. The river acted as a natural highway, allowing workers, materials, and supplies to move easily between different parts of Egypt. Large boats loaded with stones from quarries in the south traveled up and down the Nile to reach construction sites. Building projects like the pyramids required a huge amount of resources and labor, but with the Nile, the Egyptians could transport massive stones and building materials from far away, making these enormous constructions possible. The Mediterranean Sea provided access to valuable materials from other lands, such as cedarwood from Lebanon and copper from Cyprus, which were essential for Egyptian builders and craftsmen.

Egypt's location near the Mediterranean allowed the pharaohs to establish trade routes with neighboring civilizations. Trade was vital for the Egyptian economy, and Egyptian merchants sailed to the lands along the Mediterranean to exchange goods. The Egyptians exported items like grain, linen, and papyrus, a type of paper made from a plant that grew along the Nile's banks. Papyrus was highly valued by other cultures for writing, and Egyptian papyrus became a prized item across the Mediterranean. In return, Egypt imported luxury items such as ivory, incense, gold, and exotic animals, which were used in temples, palaces, and even for offerings to the gods. This exchange of goods created connections between Egypt and places like Crete, Mesopotamia, and Anatolia, making Egypt a central player in the Mediterranean world.

Many pharaohs worked hard to keep Egypt's trade routes open and safe. They built powerful navies to protect Egyptian ships from pirates and hostile forces, ensuring that goods could travel freely. The

Egyptians were skilled boat builders and created boats designed for different purposes—some for transporting goods, others for ceremonies, and some for exploring distant lands. Egypt's connection to the Mediterranean wasn't just about trade, though; it was also a way to gather information about other lands. Egyptian explorers and traders brought back stories of foreign customs, technologies, and even gods, which sometimes influenced Egyptian society. This contact with the outside world helped Egypt learn about new ideas and inventions, making its civilization even richer and more advanced.

The Mediterranean also played a role in the Egyptians' religious beliefs. The Egyptians had a deep respect for the cycles of nature, especially the yearly flooding of the Nile, which they believed was controlled by the gods. Osiris, the god of the afterlife, was closely connected to the Nile, as he was thought to be the force behind the annual floods that brought life to the land. The Egyptians believed that the Nile flowed from the underworld, connecting the living world to the realm of the dead, where Osiris ruled. The Mediterranean, as the sea into which the Nile emptied, was seen as a kind of boundary between the familiar land of Egypt and the mysterious lands beyond, where other gods and strange creatures were thought to dwell.

One of the greatest Egyptian pharaohs, Ramses II, used Egypt's connection to the Mediterranean to expand his influence. He built strong alliances with neighboring kingdoms and even led his armies into battle to protect Egypt's territories and trading routes. The famous Battle of Kadesh, where Ramses fought the Hittites, took place near the Mediterranean and was one of the largest chariot battles in history. Ramses' victory helped secure Egypt's influence in the region, and he later signed a peace treaty with the Hittites, one of the world's earliest known peace agreements. Through his actions, Ramses showed how important the Mediterranean was for Egypt's power and stability.

The Egyptian city of Alexandria, founded by Alexander the Great after he conquered Egypt, became a major center of learning and culture by the Mediterranean Sea. Alexandria housed the Great Library, where scholars from all over the world gathered to study and exchange knowledge. The city was famous for its lighthouse, one of the Seven Wonders of the Ancient World, which guided sailors safely to its shores. Although Alexandria was established after the time of the early pharaohs, it became a symbol of Egypt's importance in the Mediterranean and attracted traders, scholars, and artists from across the region. The knowledge preserved in Alexandria's library influenced generations of thinkers and helped Egypt maintain its reputation as a center of wisdom and learning.

Egypt's connection to the Mediterranean also became crucial in its interactions with powerful empires, such as Greece and Rome. Cleopatra, the last pharaoh of Egypt, had close ties with Rome, forming alliances with leaders like Julius Caesar and Mark Antony. Cleopatra used Egypt's wealth and resources to strengthen her power and maintain Egypt's independence for as long as possible. However, after her death, Egypt eventually became a province of the Roman Empire. This marked the end of the pharaohs' rule, but Egypt's legacy lived on as a crucial part of the Roman Empire, contributing its knowledge, wealth, and culture to the broader Mediterranean world.

Throughout its history, Egypt's link to the Mediterranean helped it grow from a single river-bound kingdom into a powerful civilization with influence far beyond its borders. The pharaohs' vision, the Nile's gifts, and the Mediterranean's vast waters combined to make Egypt a central part of the ancient world. The river that brought life to Egypt continued to flow into the Mediterranean, carrying Egyptian culture, ideas, and goods across the sea and leaving a lasting legacy on civilizations that came after. Egypt's unique connection to the Nile and the Mediterranean set it apart as a remarkable civilization that continues to fascinate and inspire us to this day.

Chapter 6: The Great City of Carthage

Carthage was one of the most powerful cities of the ancient world, located on the northern coast of Africa in what is now Tunisia. It was founded by the Phoenicians, a group of sea traders from the city of Tyre (in modern-day Lebanon), around 814 BCE. According to legend, Carthage was established by a princess named Elissa, also known as Dido, who fled her home in Tyre after a family dispute. Dido is said to have arrived at a spot along the North African coast and, using clever negotiations with local leaders, claimed enough land to build a small city that would eventually grow into the mighty Carthage. As the legend goes, she asked for only as much land as could be covered by an oxhide. When her request was granted, Dido cut the oxhide into long, thin strips and stretched it around a large area of land, laying the foundation for Carthage, which would become one of the most prosperous cities in the Mediterranean.

Carthage's location along the coast made it an ideal center for trade and exploration. It was strategically positioned near the narrow passage between the Mediterranean Sea and the Atlantic Ocean, which allowed the city's merchants to control trade routes throughout the region. The people of Carthage, known as Carthaginians, were skilled sailors and traders, just like their Phoenician ancestors. They sailed across the Mediterranean Sea, establishing colonies and trading posts all along the coasts of North Africa, Spain, and even as far as Sicily and Sardinia. This network allowed them to trade with many different cultures, exchanging goods like metals, textiles, spices, and precious items. Carthage grew rich from this trade, and it became one of the most powerful cities in the ancient world, rivaling even Rome.

The Carthaginians were known for their incredible skill in shipbuilding, and their navy was one of the strongest of its time. Carthaginian ships were built for speed and strength, and their designs were highly advanced. They used both oars and sails to maneuver their ships, allowing them to travel vast distances and engage in naval battles when needed. Carthage's naval power was so great that it dominated the western Mediterranean for centuries. Their navy was not only a symbol of Carthaginian strength but also a crucial tool for protecting their trading routes and colonies from pirates and rival powers. The Carthaginians were also clever strategists, using their knowledge of the sea to outmaneuver enemies and defend their territory.

Carthage was also famous for its grand harbor, which was one of the largest and most sophisticated of its time. This harbor was divided into two sections: one for merchant ships and one for the navy. The naval section was circular and could hold over two hundred warships. Each ship had its own dock, and the harbor was equipped with shipyards where ships could be repaired and maintained. This unique harbor allowed Carthage to respond quickly to threats and protected its fleet from storms and attacks. The harbor was a marvel of engineering and demonstrated Carthage's strength and organization. It also served as a hub where merchants and travelers from all over the Mediterranean gathered, bringing new goods, ideas, and influences to the city.

Carthage's wealth and success made it a target for other powerful civilizations, especially Rome. As Rome expanded its influence, it began to clash with Carthage, leading to a series of conflicts known as the Punic Wars. These wars would become some of the most famous in ancient history, filled with dramatic battles, legendary leaders, and heroic tales of bravery. The Carthaginian general Hannibal became one of the most famous military leaders in history during the Second Punic War. He was known for his daring strategy of leading his army, including war elephants, over the Alps to surprise the Romans. Hannibal's journey was incredibly dangerous, and he lost many men and animals along the way, but he managed to reach Italy and spent over a decade fighting the Romans on their own soil. Although

Hannibal won several battles, he was ultimately unable to capture Rome, and Carthage eventually lost the war.

The Punic Wars had a devastating impact on Carthage. After losing the first two wars, Carthage was weakened, and Rome imposed strict limits on its power. But despite these setbacks, Carthage managed to recover economically, and it continued to be a wealthy trading city. However, Rome still saw Carthage as a threat, and the Romans feared that the city would rise again. This led to the Third Punic War, in which Rome set out to destroy Carthage once and for all. The Roman general Scipio Aemilianus led a brutal siege against the city, and after three years, Carthage fell. The Romans destroyed the city, burning it to the ground, and reportedly sowed salt into the soil to prevent anything from growing there again. The destruction of Carthage marked the end of an era, as Rome became the dominant power in the Mediterranean.

Despite its destruction, the legacy of Carthage continued to influence the Mediterranean world. Carthaginian culture, technology, and innovations in trade and navigation were adopted by other cultures, including the Romans. The city's history and the bravery of its people, especially figures like Dido and Hannibal, continued to inspire stories, legends, and even plays for centuries. Carthage left behind a rich legacy in art, architecture, and learning, and its influence can still be felt in modern North Africa and Mediterranean cultures. Carthage's story also serves as a powerful reminder of how a small city can grow to achieve greatness, and how a civilization's influence can endure even after its physical presence is gone.

The history of Carthage shows us the power of resilience and ambition. The Carthaginians were known for their determination and ingenuity, and they achieved incredible things through their skill in trade, navigation, and military strategy. They were also deeply connected to the sea, using it to build a vast network of trade and culture that reached far beyond their own city's borders. The Mediterranean was more than just a body of water for the

Carthaginians; it was a pathway to opportunity, adventure, and connection with other cultures. Carthage was a city that thrived on exploration, wealth, and the exchange of ideas, showing us how powerful a civilization can become when it embraces both tradition and innovation.

Even though Carthage was destroyed, its ruins are still a testament to its former glory. Today, archaeologists continue to uncover pieces of Carthage's history, from its grand harbor to the remains of its temples, homes, and marketplaces. These discoveries help us understand more about the Carthaginians' way of life and the achievements of a city that once stood as a beacon of power and culture in the ancient world. Through these remnants, we get a glimpse into a time when Carthage ruled the seas and inspired awe in all who encountered it.

Chapter 7: The Minoans: Builders of a Sea Kingdom

The Minoans were one of the earliest civilizations to rise in the Mediterranean region, flourishing on the island of Crete over 4,000 years ago. This remarkable civilization thrived from around 2000 BCE to 1450 BCE and is often considered the first advanced society in Europe. The Minoans were known for their impressive achievements in art, architecture, trade, and technology. They were a peaceful people who relied on the sea for their wealth and survival, building a sea kingdom that became influential across the Mediterranean. The Minoan culture was centered around their grand palaces, lively trade networks, and a unique way of life that was closely connected to the ocean.

One of the most striking features of Minoan civilization was their grand palaces, especially the palace of Knossos, which was the largest and most famous. Knossos was a vast complex with hundreds of rooms, winding passageways, grand staircases, and courtyards. This palace was more than just a royal residence; it was the center of Minoan society, serving as a place for administrative work, religious ceremonies, storage, and even entertainment. The palace was beautifully decorated with frescoes—paintings made directly on wet plaster walls—that depicted scenes of nature, daily life, and Minoan culture. Many frescoes showed people engaging in activities like dancing, jumping over bulls, and sailing, giving us a glimpse into the lively and joyful Minoan lifestyle. The Minoans loved color, and their art was full of bright, vivid shades of blue, red, and yellow, reflecting their admiration for the world around them.

The Minoans were skilled builders and engineers. They constructed elaborate multi-story buildings with advanced plumbing systems that included running water and indoor toilets, which was incredibly advanced for their time. The palaces were built to withstand earthquakes, which were common in the region, showing how well the Minoans understood their environment. They used large stones, timber, and clay bricks to make their structures strong and durable. The palaces were designed with open courtyards and plenty of light, creating airy spaces that were comfortable in the Mediterranean climate. The Minoans' ability to construct such sophisticated buildings is one of the many reasons they are remembered as great builders.

The Minoans were also deeply connected to the sea. Living on an island, they naturally turned to the sea for resources, transportation, and trade. They built strong, sturdy ships that allowed them to travel far and wide across the Mediterranean. These ships had both sails and oars, making them fast and reliable, and the Minoans became expert sailors, navigating the open waters with skill. Through their seafaring abilities, they established extensive trade routes, exchanging goods with other civilizations like Egypt, Mesopotamia, and the Levant. Minoan merchants brought items such as olive oil, wine, wool, and pottery to trade with neighboring cultures. In return, they acquired valuable resources that were not available on Crete, like precious metals, ivory, and exotic stones. Trade brought great wealth to the Minoans, allowing them to build their impressive palaces and create stunning art.

The Minoans were known for their craftsmanship, especially in pottery and jewelry. Minoan pottery was famous for its intricate designs, often inspired by nature. The Minoans loved to decorate their pottery with images of sea creatures like octopuses, fish, and dolphins, as well as flowers and plants. Their pottery was so well-made and beautiful that it became highly sought after in other regions, spreading Minoan art and influence across the Mediterranean. Minoan jewelry was equally impressive, crafted from gold, silver, and gemstones. The Minoans made necklaces, bracelets, and rings that were not only beautiful but also showed off their skill and creativity. These items have been found in archaeological sites far beyond Crete, showing just how far Minoan culture reached.

One of the most fascinating aspects of Minoan culture was their religion. The Minoans practiced a nature-based religion that focused on gods and goddesses associated with the earth, animals, and the sea. They worshipped powerful goddesses, who were often depicted with snakes or birds, symbols of wisdom and protection. The Minoans believed that nature was sacred and that the gods and goddesses controlled the forces of the natural world, such as the weather, harvests, and the sea. Their religious ceremonies were held in sanctuaries, caves, and on mountain peaks, places they considered sacred. Some ceremonies took place in the palaces, where people would gather to honor the gods, sing, dance, and make offerings.

The bull held special significance in Minoan culture, as it was associated with strength and fertility. Minoans practiced a unique ritual known as bull-leaping, in which young men and women would grasp the horns of a bull and leap over its back. This dangerous activity was likely a part of their religious ceremonies, symbolizing courage and the Minoans' respect for nature's power. Bull-leaping is often depicted in Minoan art, and it became a lasting symbol of their civilization. The Minoans' respect for the bull was so strong that it even influenced later myths and legends, including the famous Greek myth of the Minotaur—a creature with the body of a man and the head of a bull that lived in a labyrinth on Crete.

The Minoans used a writing system known as Linear A, which has not been fully deciphered to this day. Linear A was likely used for record-keeping, documenting trade, and perhaps religious texts. Archaeologists have found clay tablets with Linear A inscriptions in the ruins of Minoan palaces, which give clues about Minoan society. However, because we cannot yet read this writing, much about Minoan life, beliefs, and history remains a mystery. The lack of written records adds to the intrigue of the Minoans, as we rely heavily on the artifacts they left behind to piece together their story.

The Minoan civilization came to a sudden end around 1450 BCE, and historians are still not entirely sure why. Some believe that a massive volcanic eruption on the nearby island of Thera (modern-day Santorini) caused the collapse of the Minoan civilization. This eruption was one of the largest in history, and it likely sent huge waves, or tsunamis, crashing into the shores of Crete, damaging ports and settlements. The ash from the eruption might have also affected the climate, leading to poor harvests and food shortages. Others think that the Minoans were invaded by people from mainland Greece, known as the Mycenaeans, who took over the island and adopted many elements of Minoan culture. Whatever the cause, the end of the Minoan civilization marked the beginning of a new era in the Mediterranean.

Although the Minoan civilization eventually disappeared, their influence continued to live on. The Mycenaeans, who became powerful after the fall of the Minoans, were heavily influenced by Minoan culture. They adopted Minoan art styles, religious practices, and even some of their trade networks, keeping Minoan culture alive in a new form. The Greeks, who followed the Mycenaeans, were also inspired by Minoan achievements, and many Greek myths and legends have connections to Minoan stories, like the myth of the Minotaur. The Minoans left a lasting legacy on the Mediterranean world, influencing art, trade, and mythology for centuries to come.

Today, the Minoans are remembered as a vibrant, peaceful civilization that achieved remarkable things through their love of the sea and their respect for nature. Archaeologists continue to uncover artifacts from Minoan sites on Crete, learning more about this fascinating culture. The Minoans' grand palaces, colorful art, and impressive skills in trade and sailing make them one of the most intriguing civilizations of the ancient Mediterranean. They remind us of a time when the Mediterranean was a bridge that connected people, ideas, and cultures, and they left a legacy that continues to inspire and captivate us today. The Minoans, with their creativity, their sea kingdom, and their mysterious end, remain one of history's great stories.

Chapter 8: The Rise and Fall of the Byzantine Empire

The Byzantine Empire, one of the most fascinating empires in history, lasted for over a thousand years, from around 330 to 1453 CE. It emerged as the eastern part of the Roman Empire, with its capital at Constantinople, a city that became one of the wealthiest and most important in the world. Constantinople, which is modern-day Istanbul, Turkey, was ideally located between Europe and Asia, making it a hub for trade, culture, and political power. The people of the Byzantine Empire saw themselves as Romans, carrying on the traditions of the Roman Empire, but their culture gradually became more Greek in language and customs. As a result, the Byzantine Empire became a unique blend of Roman government, Greek culture, and Christian religion, making it stand out as a powerful civilization in the medieval world.

The Byzantine Empire was officially founded when the Roman Emperor Constantine the Great moved the capital of the Roman Empire from Rome to the ancient city of Byzantium in 330 CE, renaming it Constantinople in his honor. Constantine made Christianity the official religion of the empire, which was a major shift from the old Roman ways, where many gods were worshipped. Christianity grew stronger in the Byzantine Empire and became a central part of Byzantine life. Churches, monasteries, and cathedrals were built all over the empire, including the grand Hagia Sophia in Constantinople, which was one of the largest and most beautiful churches in the world at the time. The Byzantines believed that their empire was divinely chosen to carry on the legacy of Rome and protect the Christian faith.

One of the greatest Byzantine emperors was Justinian I, who ruled from 527 to 565 CE. Justinian wanted to restore the Roman Empire to its former glory and spent much of his reign fighting wars to regain lands that had been lost. His general, Belisarius, led successful campaigns against the Vandals in North Africa, the Ostrogoths in Italy, and the Visigoths in Spain. For a time, Justinian managed to expand the empire's territory, bringing it closer to the size of the old Roman Empire. Justinian is also famous for creating a unified code of laws, known as the Justinian Code. This set of laws organized and clarified the many confusing laws that had developed over the centuries in the Roman Empire. The Justinian Code became the foundation for legal systems in Europe and influenced many modern laws. Under Justinian, Constantinople became even more magnificent, as he rebuilt much of the city, including the Hagia Sophia, which remains one of the most remarkable structures in the world.

Byzantine society was sophisticated and complex, with a strong economy based on trade, crafts, and agriculture. The Byzantines traded goods like silk, spices, wine, and grains, which were in high demand throughout Europe and Asia. Constantinople, located on the Bosporus Strait, controlled the sea routes between the Black Sea and the Mediterranean, giving the Byzantines great control over trade. The empire's economy was so successful that it created a gold coin called the solidus, which became a standard for trade in the Mediterranean. The Byzantine emperors managed the empire carefully, maintaining an organized government and a strong military to protect their borders.

The Byzantine military was powerful and advanced, using strategies and technologies that were ahead of their time. One of their most famous inventions was "Greek fire," a mysterious, flammable liquid that could burn even on water. Greek fire was used in naval battles to protect Constantinople from invaders, and it was a terrifying weapon that enemies feared. Byzantine soldiers were well-trained, and the empire had a system of fortified towns and castles that helped defend against attacks. The Byzantines were often under threat from different enemies, including the Persians, Arabs, and Slavs, and their ability to defend their lands helped the empire survive for centuries.

Religion was central to the Byzantine Empire, and it influenced all aspects of daily life. The Byzantines were devoted Christians, and the empire was home to many churches, monasteries, and religious scholars. However, there were disagreements within the Christian Church, leading to a major division known as the Great Schism in 1054. The Byzantine Church, or Eastern Orthodox Church, and the Western Roman Catholic Church split over differences in beliefs, practices, and authority. This separation created a lasting division between the Eastern Orthodox and Roman Catholic Churches that still exists today. Despite this split, religion continued to play a crucial role in the Byzantine Empire, with emperors and church leaders working closely together.

The Byzantine Empire faced many challenges over the centuries, including invasions and internal conflicts. In the 7th century, the empire lost large parts of its territory to the expanding Arab Islamic Caliphates, including important regions like Egypt and Syria. These losses weakened the empire, but it managed to survive by focusing on defending its remaining territories and maintaining a strong navy. The empire's economy and culture continued to thrive, especially in Constantinople, which remained a center of wealth and learning. Byzantine scholars preserved many ancient Greek and Roman texts, including works of philosophy, science, and literature, which would later be rediscovered during the Renaissance in Europe.

During the 11th and 12th centuries, the Byzantine Empire began to decline. One of the reasons for this was the rise of new enemies, such as the Seljuk Turks, who were expanding their power in Asia Minor, a region that had been the heartland of the Byzantine Empire. The Turks defeated the Byzantines in the Battle of Manzikert in 1071, which led to the loss of much of Asia Minor. This was a significant blow to the empire's resources and weakened its defenses. To make matters worse, tensions with Western Europe grew, especially as European crusaders passed through Byzantine lands on their way to the Holy Land. Although the Byzantines and the crusaders were both Christian, their relationship was often strained.

In 1204, the Fourth Crusade, which was originally intended to recapture Jerusalem, turned against Constantinople instead. The crusaders attacked and sacked the city, causing massive destruction and stealing valuable treasures. For over 50 years, Constantinople was ruled by crusaders in what is known as the Latin Empire. This occupation was a dark time for the Byzantine Empire, as much of the city's wealth and culture were lost or destroyed. The Byzantines eventually regained control of Constantinople in 1261, but the empire was a shadow of its former self, weakened and with much less territory.

In its final years, the Byzantine Empire struggled to survive against the growing power of the Ottoman Turks. The Ottomans steadily advanced into Byzantine lands, capturing key cities and territories. By the 15th century, Constantinople was all that remained of the once-great Byzantine Empire. In 1453, after a long siege, the Ottoman Sultan Mehmed II captured Constantinople, marking the end of the Byzantine Empire. The fall of Constantinople was a turning point in history, as it signaled the end of the medieval world and the beginning of the Renaissance in Europe. The Ottomans renamed the city Istanbul, and it became the capital of the Ottoman Empire.

Even though the Byzantine Empire fell, its legacy lives on. The Byzantines preserved much of the knowledge of ancient Greece and Rome, which influenced the development of Western civilization. The Eastern Orthodox Church, which started in Byzantium, still exists today and is an important part of Christian history. Byzantine art, with its iconic mosaics and religious icons, continues to inspire artists around the world. The Byzantines' achievements in law, especially through the Justinian Code, influenced legal systems for centuries. The Byzantine Empire also played a crucial role in connecting Europe and

Asia, allowing for the exchange of ideas, goods, and culture between different parts of the world.

The story of the Byzantine Empire is one of resilience, culture, and legacy. For over a thousand years, the Byzantines managed to preserve and build upon the traditions of the Roman Empire, creating a civilization that blended Roman, Greek, and Christian elements in unique ways. Their achievements in art, law, religion, and warfare helped shape the medieval world and left a lasting impact on history. The rise and fall of the Byzantine Empire remind us of the strength of empires but also of how they can be vulnerable to internal struggles and external pressures. The Byzantine Empire's legacy continues to inspire historians, scholars, and people around the world who marvel at its remarkable history and cultural richness.

Chapter 9: The Empire of Alexander the Great

The empire of Alexander the Great is one of history's most thrilling tales, filled with adventure, ambition, and a vision that stretched farther than anyone had imagined. Alexander was born in 356 BCE in a small kingdom called Macedonia, which was located in the northern part of ancient Greece. From a young age, Alexander was taught to think big. His father, King Philip II, was a brilliant military leader who dreamed of uniting the Greek city-states, which were often at war with each other, and creating a powerful, united nation. Alexander learned about warfare, leadership, and strategy from his father, but he also had an amazing teacher named Aristotle, one of the greatest philosophers of all time. Aristotle taught him about philosophy, science, literature, and culture, opening his mind to the wonders of the world and helping to prepare him for a future that was full of challenges.

When Alexander was just 20 years old, his father was assassinated, and Alexander became the king of Macedonia. He inherited his father's powerful army and his dream of expanding the kingdom. But Alexander didn't just want to unite Greece; he wanted to conquer the entire known world. He had an unbreakable determination, a love for adventure, and a deep belief that he was destined to achieve greatness. With his soldiers by his side, he set out on an extraordinary journey that would take him across thousands of miles, through deserts, mountains, and rivers, into lands that no Greek had ever seen.

Alexander's first challenge was to secure his hold over Greece. Some of the Greek city-states saw his young age and inexperience as an opportunity to rebel. But Alexander quickly showed them that he was a strong and determined leader. He defeated the rebellious city-states, and soon the whole of Greece was united under his rule. With Greece firmly under his control, Alexander turned his attention to his greatest goal: the Persian Empire. Persia was the largest and most powerful empire in the world at the time, stretching from modern-day Turkey to India. It was ruled by King Darius III, who commanded a massive army and was thought to be unbeatable. But Alexander believed he could succeed.

In 334 BCE, Alexander led his army across the Hellespont, a narrow body of water that separated Europe from Asia. As he set foot on Asian soil, he threw his spear into the ground, claiming the land as his own and declaring that his campaign was blessed by the gods. His first battle was at the Granicus River, where he faced a Persian army. Even though his forces were outnumbered, Alexander used brilliant tactics and led his soldiers fearlessly into battle, defeating the Persians. This victory was just the beginning of his incredible journey.

Alexander continued to march through Asia Minor (modern-day Turkey), winning battles and capturing cities. His most famous battle came in 333 BCE at a place called Issus, where he faced King Darius III himself. Once again, Alexander was outnumbered, but he had a strategy. He led a fierce charge straight toward Darius, causing the Persian king to flee in fear. This victory made Alexander a hero among his men and showed the world that the Persian Empire could be defeated. After Issus, Alexander marched down the Mediterranean coast, conquering the cities he encountered. He entered Egypt, where he was welcomed as a liberator since the Egyptians disliked being ruled by the Persians. In Egypt, Alexander founded a city that would carry his name, Alexandria. This city would become one of the greatest centers of learning and culture in the ancient world, home to the famous Library of Alexandria and a melting pot of Greek and Egyptian cultures.

Alexander then turned back to face Darius one last time. In 331 BCE, they met at the Battle of Gaugamela, one of the most important battles in history. Although Darius had assembled a huge army with elephants and chariots, Alexander's tactics and fearless leadership once again led him to victory. After the battle, Darius fled, leaving his empire to Alexander. Soon after, Darius was killed by his own men, and Alexander became the king of the vast Persian Empire. Alexander marched through Persia, capturing its rich cities, including Babylon, Susa, and Persepolis, the Persian capital. At Persepolis, Alexander's men burned the city, possibly as revenge for the Persian invasions of Greece years earlier, or perhaps as a sign that he had conquered Persia completely. By this point, Alexander controlled an empire larger than any before it, stretching from Greece and Egypt to the borders of India.

But Alexander was not satisfied. He wanted to push even farther east to explore lands that were unknown to the Greeks. In 327 BCE, he led his army into India, crossing the Indus River and encountering new cultures, animals, and people. In India, he faced one of his toughest opponents, King Porus, who had a powerful army that included war elephants. Alexander won the Battle of the Hydaspes River against Porus, but he was so impressed by the king's bravery and skill that he allowed him to continue ruling his kingdom as an ally. This battle marked the easternmost point of Alexander's conquests.

By this time, Alexander's men were tired and homesick. They had marched thousands of miles from home, fought in countless battles, and endured harsh conditions. They wanted to return to Greece, and Alexander finally agreed. He led his army back through the deserts of southern Persia, where they suffered greatly from hunger, thirst, and exhaustion. Many of his soldiers died on this journey, and Alexander himself became weak and ill. Despite these hardships, he managed to lead his army back to Babylon, where he planned to rule his vast empire and begin new projects, including building cities and spreading Greek culture.

But in 323 BCE, at the young age of 32, Alexander fell seriously ill and died in Babylon. The cause of his death is still a mystery, with some historians believing he was poisoned, while others think he died of a fever or a disease. His death marked the end of his incredible journey and the beginning of new challenges for his empire. Since Alexander left no clear heir, his generals, known as the Diadochi, fought among themselves for control of his empire. Eventually, the empire was divided into several smaller kingdoms, including Egypt under Ptolemy, Macedonia under Antigonus, and the Seleucid Empire in Persia.

Although Alexander's empire did not last long after his death, his legacy endured for centuries. His conquests spread Greek culture, language, and ideas across three continents, from the Mediterranean to the borders of India. This period, known as the Hellenistic Era, was a time of cultural blending and exchange. Greek ideas mixed with Persian, Egyptian, and Indian traditions, creating new forms of art, philosophy, science, and literature. The city of Alexandria in Egypt became a major center of learning, attracting scholars from around the world who studied everything from mathematics to astronomy. Even after the fall of his empire, Alexander's impact continued to shape the ancient world.

Alexander was admired for his courage, leadership, and vision, but he was also seen as ruthless and demanding. He expected total loyalty from his men and often punished those who opposed him. He was known for his fierce temper and his unyielding drive to succeed. Yet, he inspired his soldiers to follow him to the ends of the earth, and he achieved feats that seemed impossible. People began to see him as a god-like figure, a legend who had dared to conquer the unknown. Stories of his adventures became popular, and he was remembered as one of the greatest military leaders in history.

Alexander's life and achievements continue to capture the imagination of people today. He showed the world what could be accomplished with bravery, determination, and vision. His empire brought different cultures together and laid the foundation for a new era of learning and exploration. While his empire may have been short-lived, his influence on history was long-lasting, as he changed the course of civilizations and connected distant lands in a way that had never been done before. Alexander the Great remains a symbol of ambition, adventure, and the enduring power of dreams.

Chapter 10: Pirates of the Mediterranean

The Mediterranean Sea was once a bustling highway for pirates, who ruled the waves and struck fear into the hearts of sailors, merchants, and coastal cities. These weren't the pirates of the Caribbean you might picture with parrots on their shoulders and treasure maps in hand, but they were every bit as daring and dangerous. For centuries, the Mediterranean was a hotspot for pirate activity, attracting people from many different backgrounds, from soldiers and rebels to adventurers and outlaws. They were known for their cunning, courage, and sometimes cruelty, as they raided ships, seized goods, and even captured people to sell as slaves.

Pirates had many reasons for setting sail in the Mediterranean. Some were simply looking for a way to survive in a world where life was tough, and others saw it as an opportunity to get rich quickly. The Mediterranean was a prime spot for piracy because it was a major trade route connecting Europe, Africa, and Asia. Ships filled with goods like spices, silk, gold, and silver traveled through its waters, making them attractive targets for pirates. These pirates, often skilled sailors themselves, would wait along busy trade routes, watching for merchant ships to come their way. Once they spotted their prey, they would chase it down, using their fast and nimble ships to their advantage.

Different types of pirates operated in the Mediterranean, each with their unique style and motives. There were Greek pirates who raided the coastlines and islands, especially during times when Greece was divided into warring city-states, which left some areas vulnerable. There were also the Cilician pirates, who became notorious for their daring attacks on Roman ships. Cilicia, a coastal region in present-day Turkey, was a pirate haven where fleets of pirate ships could hide among the rocky shores. The Cilician pirates were so powerful that they even captured high-ranking Roman citizens and held them for ransom. In fact, the famous Roman general Julius Caesar was once captured by these pirates as a young man. While they held him hostage, Caesar reportedly promised them he would hunt them down once he was free – and he did exactly that, returning with a fleet to punish them after his release.

One of the most famous and feared groups of pirates in the Mediterranean were the Barbary pirates. These pirates came from the North African coast, along what was known as the Barbary Coast, which included present-day Morocco, Algeria, Tunisia, and Libya. They were known for their swift ships and ruthless tactics, and they often attacked European ships, as well as towns and villages along the coast. The Barbary pirates were different from other pirates in that they were often supported by local rulers who allowed them to operate in exchange for a share of their loot. These rulers saw piracy as a way to make money and gain power, so they encouraged it. The Barbary pirates were especially feared because they didn't just take goods; they captured people, too, often selling them into slavery. Many Europeans who lived along the coast feared being taken in a surprise raid and sold in the markets of North Africa.

The Barbary pirates also had a special name for their leaders – they were called "corsairs." The corsairs were often well-organized and operated under a form of government permission known as a "letter of marque." This meant they were considered "legal" pirates because they had permission from their rulers to attack certain ships, especially those from rival countries. In this way, the Barbary pirates were different from other pirates, who operated outside of any government's control. Corsairs were like a mix between pirates and privateers (sailors hired by a government to attack enemy ships). This practice of legal piracy meant that the Barbary corsairs were sometimes involved in conflicts between European nations and the Muslim states of North Africa. Over time, the European powers grew tired of the Barbary pirates' attacks, leading to wars and treaties aimed at ending their raids.

Life as a Mediterranean pirate was hard and dangerous. Pirates were constantly on the move, sailing from one place to another, often living in cramped and uncomfortable conditions aboard their ships. Their ships were usually small, but very fast, making it easier to escape from larger enemy ships. Pirates also needed to be skilled navigators and sailors, as the Mediterranean Sea was full of rocky coastlines, islands, and hidden reefs. The pirates would sail close to the coast, often using the cover of night or mist to hide their approach. They knew the waters well, which gave them an advantage over the merchants and sailors who were just passing through.

Pirate attacks were usually quick and fierce. The pirates would sail up to a merchant ship, fire their cannons or throw grappling hooks to bring the ship close, and then jump aboard with weapons in hand. They often used swords, daggers, and pistols, scaring the merchant crew into surrendering. Once on board, they would take anything valuable – food, money, spices, or textiles. Sometimes, if the merchant ship was too damaged to sail, they would take it with them to add to their fleet. Pirates were often ruthless, but they were also clever, using disguises or even pretending to be friendly traders to lure other ships close before attacking.

While piracy was profitable for some, it also had its risks. Pirates faced not only the dangers of the sea but also the threat of being captured by naval forces. Many Mediterranean powers, such as the Romans, Egyptians, and later the Venetians and Ottomans, fought hard to protect their trade routes from pirates. They would send out powerful fleets to chase down and capture pirate ships. Pirates who were caught were usually punished severely. Some were forced into slavery, while others were executed as a warning to others. Despite these risks, piracy continued because the potential for riches was too tempting for many.

Pirate life wasn't all about raiding and fighting, though. When not at sea, pirates would sometimes hide out in secret coves or on islands.

They would spend their loot in pirate havens, towns where pirates could come and go without fear of being arrested. These havens were often bustling with activity, full of traders, craftsmen, and other pirates who came to relax, repair their ships, and sell or trade their stolen goods. Some pirate havens in the Mediterranean became almost like small pirate kingdoms, where the pirates ruled themselves and had their own rules and customs.

One famous pirate haven in the Mediterranean was the island of Malta, which at times became a base for pirates, particularly during the times when European and Ottoman forces were fighting for control of the region. The knights of Malta, known as the Knights Hospitaller, were also involved in piracy. They fought against the Barbary corsairs and sometimes acted like pirates themselves, capturing Muslim ships and taking their goods. This made the Mediterranean a place of constant rivalry, with pirates and corsairs on both sides attacking each other's ships and raiding each other's coasts.

Despite their reputation for violence and theft, pirates had a kind of rough code of honor. They valued loyalty among their crew, and many pirate ships operated as democracies, where the crew voted on important decisions, like who would lead them or where they would go next. Pirates often shared the loot equally, which was different from most naval ships, where the captains and officers kept most of the money. This sense of equality attracted people to piracy who might not have found such freedom elsewhere.

Eventually, the golden age of Mediterranean piracy began to fade. As the European empires grew stronger, they sent out more powerful fleets to patrol the Mediterranean and protect their trade routes. Treaties were signed, and navies worked together to capture or kill the pirates who had once ruled the waves. By the 19th century, the Barbary pirates, in particular, faced serious opposition from both the United States and European countries, who were determined to stop their attacks once and for all. The Barbary Wars, fought by the United

States against the Barbary States, played a big role in ending the power of the Barbary corsairs.

Even though Mediterranean piracy came to an end, the stories of these daring pirates have lived on. The pirates of the Mediterranean were part of a thrilling and dangerous world, where adventure and risk were constant companions. Their stories remind us of a time when the seas were wild and untamed, and people from all over the region came together in pursuit of fortune, freedom, or just a different way of life. The Mediterranean pirates were as much a part of the region's history as the empires and civilizations that tried to control them. Today, their legacy lives on in the tales of bravery, cunning, and freedom that they left behind.

Chapter 11: The Wonders of the Egyptian Pyramids by the Sea

The Egyptian pyramids are among the most incredible achievements of the ancient world, standing as breathtaking symbols of mystery, power, and devotion. Although not directly on the Mediterranean coast, the pyramids rise from the desert near the Nile River, which flows into the Mediterranean. For the ancient Egyptians, the Nile wasn't just a source of life and resources; it was a bridge between their land and the rest of the Mediterranean world. The pyramids, especially the Great Pyramids of Giza, are some of the oldest and most astonishing structures in the world, built thousands of years ago. These stone giants have survived wars, invasions, and the harsh desert climate, becoming an everlasting part of Egypt's landscape and history. Even today, they inspire wonder and curiosity among people from all over the world.

Ancient Egyptians believed in a powerful afterlife, and for them, death was only the beginning of a new journey. The pyramids were built to serve as massive tombs for their pharaohs, who were considered gods on Earth. They believed that after a pharaoh died, he would journey to the afterlife, but he would need his body, his possessions, and a secure place to rest. That's where the pyramids came in. They weren't just graves; they were like magical stairways to the heavens, carefully designed to help the pharaoh reach the realm of the gods. The Egyptians believed that as long as the pyramid stood and the pharaoh's body was protected, his spirit would continue to watch over Egypt, blessing the land and its people.

Building a pyramid was no small task. It required enormous amounts of planning, resources, and manpower. The stones used to build the Great Pyramid of Giza, the largest and most famous of all, weighed several tons each, and there were millions of them! To move these massive stones, the Egyptians used ramps, sledges, and lots of skilled workers. It's believed that thousands of people, from farmers and craftsmen to architects and laborers, worked on each pyramid. Contrary to popular belief, they were not slaves but skilled workers and proud Egyptians who believed they were serving their gods and their country. Many workers even lived in nearby villages built just for them, where they were provided with food, shelter, and medical care, which was remarkable for that time.

Each pyramid was built with incredible precision, and the Great Pyramid was especially impressive. It was the tallest man-made structure in the world for over 3,800 years! Even today, scientists and historians are amazed by the engineering skill that went into constructing it. The pyramid's base is a perfect square, and each side is aligned almost exactly with the four cardinal directions – north, south, east, and west. How the Egyptians managed this without modern technology is still a mystery that baffles researchers. Some believe they used the stars, particularly the North Star, to achieve this alignment. It's a reminder that the ancient Egyptians were not only skilled builders but also expert astronomers who understood the movements of the stars and planets.

The pyramids were carefully designed to protect the pharaoh's body and his treasures from grave robbers. Inside the Great Pyramid, for instance, there are long passageways and hidden chambers that were meant to confuse intruders. The pharaoh's burial chamber, deep within the pyramid, was sealed with heavy stones to prevent anyone from getting inside. Although most of the pyramids were eventually looted over the centuries, their design still shows how much care and thought the Egyptians put into protecting their king in the afterlife. They believed that everything placed in the pyramid – from golden treasures and jewelry to food, clothing, and even board games – would help the pharaoh live comfortably in his next life. The Egyptians believed in surrounding the deceased with what they would need to enjoy the afterlife, showing how deeply they valued life after death.

The pyramids aren't the only marvels of ancient Egypt; they're part of a larger complex that included temples, statues, and smaller pyramids for queens and other important people. The Great Sphinx of Giza, a giant statue with the body of a lion and the head of a pharaoh, sits near the pyramids. The Sphinx itself is a wonder, carved from a single piece of limestone, and it guards the area like a silent sentinel. It's thought to represent the strength of a lion combined with the wisdom of a pharaoh, standing as a guardian of the pharaohs' tombs and the mysteries they hold. The Sphinx has stood for thousands of years, enduring the wind and sand of the desert, and yet it still stands proudly, keeping watch over the pyramids and the ancient land of Egypt.

The pyramids also hold secrets about ancient Egyptian society and culture. For example, the intricate carvings and inscriptions found in many of the tombs and nearby temples tell us about the Egyptian way of life, their gods, their beliefs, and their achievements. The walls of the burial chambers often show scenes of the pharaoh in the afterlife, surrounded by gods like Osiris, the god of the underworld, and Ra, the sun god. These images were meant to guide the pharaoh's soul to the afterlife, showing him the way to reach the gods and find his place among them. Some walls are decorated with hieroglyphs, the ancient Egyptian writing system, which tells stories of the pharaoh's life and deeds. These inscriptions give us a glimpse into the minds and hearts of the people who built the pyramids and the beliefs that shaped their world.

The pyramids aren't just fascinating because of their size or design; they're also valuable for what they reveal about the ancient Egyptians' scientific and mathematical knowledge. The ancient Egyptians had a remarkable understanding of geometry and measurement, which helped them build structures as enormous and precise as the pyramids. They used a system of ropes and wooden tools to measure and calculate angles, and they were able to divide the land around the Nile into perfect plots for farming. This mathematical skill was essential for constructing the pyramids, ensuring that each stone was placed in exactly the right spot. The Egyptians' expertise in mathematics and astronomy helped them create a civilization that was incredibly advanced for its time, and the pyramids are a testament to their skill and intelligence.

Over time, the pyramids have become symbols of Egypt and the wonders of the ancient world. They represent the ingenuity, faith, and dedication of the Egyptian people. Even though they were built thousands of years ago, they continue to capture the imagination of people around the world. The pyramids remind us of the power of human creativity and the lengths people will go to honor their beliefs and their leaders. They stand as monuments to a civilization that valued the journey to the afterlife as much as life itself. Today, people from all over the world come to see the pyramids and marvel at the accomplishments of a society that rose along the banks of the Nile.

As time goes on, scientists continue to study the pyramids, learning new things about how they were built and what they mean. In recent years, archaeologists have discovered hidden chambers within the Great Pyramid using advanced scanning technology. These discoveries show that the pyramids still have secrets waiting to be uncovered, mysteries that may reveal even more about the ancient Egyptians and their world. The pyramids remind us that history is always unfolding and that there are still wonders waiting to be discovered.

The Egyptian pyramids near the Mediterranean are more than just buildings; they're timeless symbols of a civilization that reached remarkable heights. The pharaohs may be long gone, but the pyramids keep their memory alive. They tell the story of a people who dared to dream big and built structures that would last through the ages. Standing beneath the blazing Egyptian sun, the pyramids continue to guard the secrets of the past, connecting us to a time when gods walked among mortals and the journey to the afterlife was just as important as the journey through life itself. These ancient wonders remind us of the greatness of ancient Egypt and the enduring legacy of a civilization that has shaped human history in countless ways.

Chapter 12: The First Sea Explorers

Long before people could fly across the globe or sail on giant cruise ships, there were brave explorers who dared to venture into the unknown seas. These first sea explorers, hailing from many ancient cultures, set off on legendary journeys that took them to faraway lands, often with only the stars and waves as their guides. Their voyages were full of mystery, excitement, and often danger. These explorers didn't have maps or GPS; instead, they relied on their knowledge of the wind, waves, and sky. Their journeys helped connect different parts of the world, spread knowledge and culture, and paved the way for future explorers who would continue to unlock the secrets of the seas.

Among the earliest known seafaring explorers were the Polynesians, who lived on islands scattered across the vast Pacific Ocean. Using only canoes, they traveled incredible distances, often without being able to see land for days or even weeks. Their boats were simple yet strong, with two hulls for balance, allowing them to navigate through strong waves and unpredictable weather. They were skilled navigators, trained to notice even the smallest changes in wind and ocean currents. By observing birds, cloud formations, and the color of the water, they could tell when land was nearby. The Polynesians are believed to have explored and settled many islands, including Hawaii, New Zealand, and Easter Island, all without modern technology. They had a tradition of storytelling and would pass down knowledge of the sea and the islands from one generation to the next, making sure each explorer knew how to find their way back home.

In the Mediterranean, the Phoenicians were known as some of the first great sea traders and explorers. They came from a region that is now part of Lebanon and were famous for their beautiful purple dye and skilled craftsmanship. The Phoenicians sailed throughout the Mediterranean, setting up trade routes and establishing colonies in places as far as North Africa and Spain. Their ships were sturdy, built to carry large amounts of goods, and they became experts in navigating the Mediterranean's sometimes treacherous waters. They also used landmarks and learned to navigate by the stars, which helped them travel at night. The Phoenicians were not only explorers but also inventors. They are credited with creating one of the first alphabets, which made it easier to record trade transactions and keep track of their journeys. Because of their adventurous spirit and trading skills, they helped spread knowledge and goods across the Mediterranean, connecting different cultures in ways that had never been done before.

Another great ancient explorer was Pytheas, a Greek sailor and geographer from the city of Massalia, which is now known as Marseille, France. Around 300 BCE, Pytheas set out on a journey to explore the Atlantic Ocean, traveling farther than most Greeks of his time. His journey took him to places that were unknown to many, including what is believed to be the British Isles and perhaps even Iceland. Pytheas described lands of endless daylight and icy seas, which were probably the polar regions. He observed natural phenomena that were unfamiliar to him, like the northern lights and the midnight sun, where the sun doesn't set for a long time. Although many people at the time didn't believe his stories, Pytheas' journey was remarkable for its time, and he is remembered as one of the first Greeks to venture beyond the familiar Mediterranean and explore the mysteries of the Atlantic.

The Vikings, hailing from Scandinavia, were another group of legendary sea explorers. They lived around 1,000 years ago and became famous for their incredible longships, which were narrow and swift, designed to navigate both open seas and shallow rivers. The Vikings didn't just raid; they also explored and settled new lands, reaching places as far away as Greenland and even North America. They called their landing spot in North America "Vinland," and it's believed they may have reached parts of present-day Canada. The Vikings navigated by the stars and also used a sunstone, a crystal that helped them determine the sun's position even on cloudy days. They were fearless sailors, braving icy waters and harsh weather as they explored lands unknown to other Europeans. The Viking's adventurous spirit and exploration skills made them one of the most successful and widespread cultures in medieval Europe.

In the Indian Ocean, traders from the Arabian Peninsula, East Africa, and India were also early sea explorers. These sailors used the monsoon winds, which change direction with the seasons, to travel long distances across the Indian Ocean. They built strong ships known as dhows, which had triangular sails designed to catch the wind from any direction, allowing them to navigate the vast ocean. These early traders brought goods like spices, silk, and precious stones, connecting the Arabian Peninsula and East Africa to India and even as far as Southeast Asia. The sailors in this region developed navigation skills that helped them journey across the Indian Ocean, and their trade routes helped spread ideas, languages, and cultures, creating a rich and diverse network of trade and culture along the coasts they visited.

The Chinese were also remarkable sea explorers, particularly during the Ming Dynasty. The most famous of these explorers was Admiral Zheng He, who led enormous fleets on voyages that took him as far as Africa, the Middle East, and Southeast Asia. Zheng He's ships were enormous, many times the size of the European ships of that time, and they carried thousands of people, including sailors, soldiers, and diplomats. His fleet included more than 300 ships, and each journey was like a floating city traveling across the ocean. Zheng He's voyages were peaceful missions, meant to show the power of China and to establish good relationships with other nations. He brought gifts from the Emperor, including silk, porcelain, and tea, and returned with treasures, animals, and people from the lands he visited. His journeys are remembered as a symbol of China's naval power and its reach across the known world.

These early explorers changed the world in ways they might not have realized at the time. By traveling into unknown waters, they opened new pathways for trade, which brought different cultures and civilizations into contact with one another. They shared ideas, customs, and technologies, which led to advancements in science, mathematics, and art across many regions. Many of the routes they discovered and established later became important pathways for trade and exploration, influencing the world for centuries to come. These explorers also helped shape our understanding of the world. Before their journeys, people's knowledge of geography was limited. Through their travels, they discovered new lands, mapped coastlines, and found ways to navigate using the stars, winds, and ocean currents. Each journey contributed a little more to the picture of the world as we know it.

The bravery and curiosity of these early explorers have left an everlasting mark on history. They ventured into dangerous and uncharted waters with only a desire to see what lay beyond the horizon. Their stories continue to inspire us to explore, learn, and connect with people from all over the world. These first sea explorers set an example of courage and adventure, showing that the world is full of wonders waiting to be discovered. Their journeys remind us that exploration is about more than just reaching a destination; it's about the curiosity, determination, and willingness to face the unknown that drive us to discover new horizons.

Chapter 13: The Mythical Creatures of Mediterranean Waters

The Mediterranean Sea is not only famous for its beautiful blue waters, bustling ports, and ancient cities, but it's also a place rich in tales of mythical creatures. These creatures, born from the imagination of the people who lived along its shores, are a mix of wonder, danger, and magic. Sailors, traders, and explorers who braved the Mediterranean's waves often returned with stories of strange beings lurking in the depths, inspiring myths and legends that have been told for thousands of years. These creatures weren't just made-up characters for stories; they were a way for people to explain the unknown mysteries of the sea, a place that could be both friend and foe. Some of these creatures protected the waters, while others brought terror to anyone who crossed their paths. Let's dive into the stories of some of the most famous mythical creatures believed to roam the Mediterranean.

One of the most famous creatures of the Mediterranean is the mermaid, known as a "siren" in Greek mythology. Sirens were said to be beautiful half-human, half-fish creatures with long flowing hair and enchanting voices. But don't let their beauty fool you! Sirens were known for luring sailors toward dangerous rocks and underwater caves with their haunting songs. Once the sailors heard their singing, they would become entranced, losing all control over their ships. Often, these ships would crash, leading to the sailors' doom. Ancient Greek sailors believed that sirens lived on rocky islands, waiting to sing their songs to those who dared to come too close. The most famous story of the sirens comes from Homer's *Odyssey*, where the hero Odysseus encounters them on his long journey home. Odysseus, clever as he was, plugged his crew's ears with beeswax so they couldn't hear the sirens' voices. But he wanted to hear the song himself, so he tied himself to the mast of his ship, ordering his men not to let him go no matter what he said. This clever trick saved him, and he became one of the few who ever survived the sirens' call.

Another mysterious creature believed to roam the Mediterranean is the sea serpent. Sea serpents were imagined as massive, snake-like creatures with scaly skin, sharp teeth, and a terrifying appetite. Stories of sea serpents were popular among ancient Greek, Roman, and Phoenician sailors, who would sometimes claim to have seen giant shadows or felt strange movements in the water, especially during storms. Unlike today, where we have a better understanding of sea animals, ancient sailors didn't know what lay beneath the waves. A splash, a shadow, or even an unusually large fish could fuel their fears and imaginations. Some ancient stories even described sea serpents as protectors of underwater treasures or ancient ruins, while others depicted them as beasts who attacked ships, coiling around them and dragging them down to the depths. In these tales, defeating a sea serpent often required the courage and strength of a hero or the intervention of a god.

The hippocampus is another fantastic creature from Mediterranean mythology. Imagine a creature with the front half of a horse and the tail of a fish! The hippocampus was believed to pull the chariot of Poseidon, the Greek god of the sea. In art and literature, the hippocampus is often shown as a graceful creature, leaping out of the water with its horse-like front legs while its fishy tail swirls below. The Greeks saw the hippocampus as a noble and loyal creature, a kind of "sea steed" that served the god of the ocean. Statues and paintings of the hippocampus can still be found in ruins of ancient cities around the Mediterranean, showing how much the people of that time admired this mythical creature. Some believed the hippocampus would come to the aid of sailors in distress, guiding them to safety or even fighting off dangerous sea creatures. This legend gave people hope and comfort as they faced the unpredictable dangers of the sea.

Scylla and Charybdis were two terrifying sea monsters who guarded the narrow passage of water between Italy and Sicily, known as the Strait of Messina. According to Greek mythology, Scylla was once a beautiful nymph, but a jealous sorceress cursed her and transformed her into a monster with twelve dog-like heads and sharp, poisonous fangs. Scylla hid among the rocks on one side of the strait, waiting to snatch sailors who sailed too close to her. On the other side of the strait was Charybdis, a powerful whirlpool that would suck in entire ships, spinning them around and dragging them down into the dark depths. Together, these two monsters made it nearly impossible to sail through the strait unharmed. In Homer's *Odyssey*, Odysseus had to navigate between these two dangers. He chose to sail closer to Scylla, deciding it was better to risk losing a few men than to have his entire ship swallowed by Charybdis. The phrase "between Scylla and Charybdis" has since become a way to describe being stuck between two difficult choices, both of which are dangerous.

In addition to these terrifying creatures, the Mediterranean was also thought to be home to nymphs, who were gentle, nature-loving spirits of the sea and rivers. Sea nymphs, known as "Nereids," were believed to be the daughters of Nereus, the old man of the sea, and they often helped sailors by calming storms or guiding them through dangerous waters. Unlike sirens, Nereids were seen as kind and helpful beings, sometimes appearing as young maidens with flowing hair and shimmering, sea-blue dresses. The Nereids were also known to accompany Poseidon, riding on dolphins or swimming gracefully by his side. Sailors prayed to these nymphs for safe travels, leaving offerings by the shore or in small shrines, hoping the Nereids would hear their pleas and protect them from harm.

Another famous mythical creature associated with the Mediterranean was the Kraken. Although the Kraken legend is more commonly associated with Norse mythology, similar tales of giant, ship-crushing creatures have been told along the Mediterranean for centuries. The Kraken was said to be an enormous squid-like creature with long, powerful tentacles. This beast would lurk below the surface, waiting for an unsuspecting ship to pass by. Then, it would rise up, wrapping its massive tentacles around the vessel, crushing it, and dragging it into the depths. While scientists today know that giant squids do exist, the Kraken of legend was far larger and much more dangerous, inspiring fear and caution among seafarers. For many, the Kraken symbolized the unpredictability of the sea and the mysterious creatures that might be hiding just out of sight.

There were also stories of sea dragons, magical creatures that were believed to have scales as strong as armor and the ability to breathe fire or create storms with their roars. These dragons, sometimes called "drakons" in Greek mythology, were believed to live in underwater caves or on lonely islands. They were often seen as protectors of hidden treasures or sacred places, and encountering a sea dragon was considered both a blessing and a curse. Heroes who defeated these dragons were seen as incredibly brave, and their stories became legendary. In some myths, sea dragons guarded ancient ruins or enchanted islands, attacking anyone who dared approach. They were respected and feared by sailors, who would avoid areas where these dragons were said to live.

The waters of the Mediterranean, filled with hidden caves, rocky cliffs, and shifting tides, provided the perfect setting for all these mythical creatures to exist in the minds of ancient people. Each creature symbolized different aspects of the sea – its beauty, its mystery, its danger, and its power. These creatures taught ancient seafarers to respect the ocean, for while it offered routes for trade and exploration, it was also a place of unpredictable forces that could change a journey in an instant. In a way, these myths were early warnings, reminding sailors to stay cautious and prepared, to be alert to the signs of changing weather, and to remember that not everything could be controlled.

These stories of mythical creatures have been passed down through generations and are still shared today, reminding us of the wonders and mysteries of the sea. While modern science has explained many of the phenomena that once inspired these myths, the creatures themselves continue to capture our imagination, inspiring books, movies, and art. They remind us of a time when the world was a vast, mysterious place and the Mediterranean Sea was a gateway to adventure and the unknown. Just as sailors once looked out across the horizon, wondering what mythical beings might be lurking beneath the waves, we, too, can let our imaginations run wild, dreaming of the mysterious creatures that might still be waiting in the deep, blue waters of the Mediterranean.

Chapter 14: Ancient Shipbuilding and the Art of Sailing

In the ancient Mediterranean world, shipbuilding and the art of sailing were skills that determined whether people could trade, explore, and wage war across the sea. Ships were not just vehicles for moving from one place to another; they were marvels of human ingenuity and symbols of power. Building a ship was a complex task that required knowledge of woodcraft, mathematics, and the behavior of the sea. Learning to sail that ship was another challenge, as sailors had to understand the wind, waves, and stars to navigate across the open water. Ancient Mediterranean societies, from the Egyptians and Phoenicians to the Greeks and Romans, each developed their own styles of ships and methods of sailing, but all shared the same goal: to master the mighty Mediterranean Sea.

The earliest ships in the Mediterranean were simple boats, often made from reeds or planks bound together with rope. In ancient Egypt, for example, reed boats made from the papyrus plant were used to travel up and down the Nile River. These boats were small and light, designed for short trips and smooth waters, but they laid the foundation for future shipbuilding. As the Egyptians began trading with nearby lands, they needed stronger ships that could handle the open sea. They soon learned to use wood from trees like cedar, which was strong and could be shaped into sturdy hulls. Their ships became larger and more complex, with sails to catch the wind and oars to help steer. These early Egyptian ships were some of the first to explore the Mediterranean, and they connected Egypt to places like Crete and Lebanon, bringing back exotic goods and stories of foreign lands.

The Phoenicians were perhaps the greatest shipbuilders and sailors of the ancient Mediterranean. Living along the coast of what is now Lebanon, the Phoenicians had easy access to the sea and a natural talent for exploration. They quickly became famous for their impressive ships, which were designed for speed, strength, and long voyages. Phoenician ships were built using a method called "shell-first" construction, where the outer hull was built first, and the inside frame was added afterward. This technique made their ships incredibly strong and able to withstand rough waves. The Phoenicians used cedar wood, which was both durable and resistant to water, allowing their ships to last longer and sail farther. With these ships, the Phoenicians traveled all around the Mediterranean, trading goods like purple dye, glass, and metals. They reached as far as Spain and North Africa, and some even believe they sailed beyond the Mediterranean into the Atlantic Ocean. Their mastery of shipbuilding and sailing helped them establish a vast trade network and earn the title of the "masters of the sea."

The Greeks took shipbuilding and sailing to new heights, especially as they began exploring and establishing colonies throughout the Mediterranean. Greek ships were designed not only for trade but also for war. One of the most famous Greek warships was the trireme, a powerful vessel with three rows of oars on each side. The trireme was fast, maneuverable, and equipped with a large bronze ram at the front, used to smash into enemy ships. It took about 170 rowers to power a trireme, and these rowers had to work together in perfect unison to keep the ship balanced and moving swiftly. Greek sailors were also skilled navigators, using the stars and coastline to guide their way. They developed charts and maps to help them remember the positions of islands and ports, and they learned to read the winds and currents. With their ships, the Greeks explored as far as Italy, North Africa, and Asia Minor, spreading their culture and influence across the Mediterranean.

The art of sailing was just as important as the ships themselves. Sailors had to understand how to read the wind, which was not an easy task in the Mediterranean. The sea was known for its unpredictable winds and sudden storms, which could catch sailors off guard. Ancient sailors used sails to harness the wind, adjusting them to change direction or speed. They also relied on oars, especially when the wind died down or they needed to make precise movements. Steering was done with a large wooden rudder, usually placed at the back of the ship. Experienced sailors could feel the movement of the waves and the wind, sensing when to make adjustments to keep the ship steady. Navigation was a challenge too, as there were no compasses or GPS systems. Instead, sailors used the stars to find their way, especially at night. The North Star, in particular, was a reliable guide for finding north, and by knowing their direction, sailors could keep their course across the open water.

The Romans, who later ruled the Mediterranean, also made great advancements in shipbuilding and sailing. They built a powerful navy to protect their empire, which stretched across the Mediterranean. Roman ships were influenced by the designs of the Greeks and the Phoenicians, but they added their own innovations. One of the most important Roman inventions was the "corvus," a large boarding plank with spikes, used to board enemy ships during battle. This allowed Roman soldiers to turn sea battles into hand-to-hand combat, where they excelled. Roman trade ships, on the other hand, were larger and could carry more cargo than ever before. These ships transported goods like grain, olive oil, and wine all across the Mediterranean, feeding the empire's cities and armies. Roman sailors, like their Greek predecessors, were skilled navigators and learned to read the sea and sky to avoid danger. They built lighthouses along the coast to guide ships safely into port, and they established a network of ports and harbors to support their vast trading system.

Shipbuilding was not just about the materials and techniques; it was also about craftsmanship and tradition. In many ancient cultures, shipbuilders passed down their knowledge from generation to generation, teaching young apprentices the skills needed to create a seaworthy vessel. Shipbuilding required a deep understanding of wood, metal, and rope, as well as knowledge of geometry and balance. Builders had to shape each piece of wood carefully, making sure the hull was strong enough to hold together under the pressure of the waves. They used pitch, a sticky substance made from tree sap, to seal the gaps between planks and make the ship waterproof. Ropes made from fibers like flax and hemp were woven tightly to create sails and rigging. Each part of the ship had to work in harmony, from the hull and sails to the rudder and oars. Shipbuilding was considered an art, and a well-built ship was a source of pride for the community.

Despite the incredible skill and craftsmanship of ancient shipbuilders, sailing the Mediterranean was still a risky endeavor. Storms could appear suddenly, bringing powerful winds and huge waves that could smash a ship to pieces. Pirates roamed the sea, ready to attack vulnerable vessels and steal their cargo. Ships could also run aground on hidden reefs or rocky shores, especially in unfamiliar waters. To reduce these risks, sailors often traveled close to the coast, stopping at ports along the way. They also sailed in groups, known as convoys, for added protection. Skilled captains knew the safest routes and the best times of year to travel, and they prepared for emergencies by carrying extra supplies and repairing tools. Despite the dangers, the rewards of the sea were too great to resist, and ancient sailors continued to venture out, driven by the promise of riches, adventure, and discovery.

Over time, shipbuilding and sailing transformed the Mediterranean from a barrier into a bridge, connecting distant lands and cultures. The sea became a highway for the exchange of goods, ideas, and people, shaping the history of the entire region. The skills and techniques developed by ancient shipbuilders and sailors laid the foundation for future generations, who would eventually sail beyond the Mediterranean to explore even greater oceans. Ancient ships were the first step in a journey that would lead to the discovery of new continents and the age of exploration. Today, the ruins of ancient shipwrecks and the stories of legendary sailors remind us of a time when the Mediterranean was the center of a vast and vibrant world, where the art of shipbuilding and the courage of sailors changed history forever.

Chapter 15: The Mediterranean's Role in Spreading Ideas

The Mediterranean Sea, more than just a vast stretch of water, has played an extraordinary role in the spread of ideas, shaping the cultures and beliefs of civilizations around it for thousands of years. This unique body of water connected distant lands like a network, allowing people from different backgrounds to exchange stories, knowledge, technology, and beliefs. Through trade routes and maritime journeys, the Mediterranean became the heart of an ancient information highway, where ideas traveled as easily as goods. From the earliest societies like the Egyptians and Phoenicians to the great empires of Greece and Rome, each culture shared something unique, and the entire region became richer in knowledge and diversity because of it.

In ancient times, people living along the Mediterranean coasts began to trade with each other. Goods like olive oil, wine, pottery, and spices were common, but something else was also being "traded"—knowledge and new ideas. As merchants sailed from one port to another, they shared stories, techniques, and even beliefs. For instance, a merchant from Egypt who knew about how to measure time using a water clock might share that knowledge with a trader from Greece, who could take it back home and adapt it. Ideas that started in one culture didn't just stay there; they were constantly spreading, changing, and mixing with other cultures as they moved across the sea.

Religions and philosophies were some of the most powerful ideas spread through the Mediterranean. The Egyptians had complex beliefs about gods, the afterlife, and the soul. Greek traders who interacted with the Egyptians might hear about these beliefs and take those ideas back to Greece, where they would inspire new stories and gods. Later, the Greeks themselves developed ideas about philosophy, questioning life's big questions like "What is truth?" and "What makes a good life?"

These philosophical ideas spread quickly across the Mediterranean, especially as more people came to admire famous Greek thinkers like Socrates, Plato, and Aristotle. These ideas even influenced the Romans, who admired Greek thought so much that they adopted much of Greek culture, art, and literature.

One of the most remarkable examples of the spread of ideas in the Mediterranean was the development and spread of democracy. In ancient Greece, the idea that ordinary citizens could have a say in their government was revolutionary. This system was not common in most other places, where kings or pharaohs ruled by birthright. Athens, a city-state in Greece, became famous for its democracy, where citizens could vote on important issues. Although not everyone had the right to vote, it was still an important step toward the idea of government by the people. When Greek culture spread, so did the idea of democracy. As other cultures in the Mediterranean learned about Greek governance, they began to think about the role of citizens in society, sparking discussions and influencing governments far beyond Greece.

The spread of writing systems was another huge development made possible by the Mediterranean. Early civilizations like the Egyptians had their own unique scripts, including the famous hieroglyphics. The Phoenicians, however, developed one of the first alphabets, which used symbols to represent sounds rather than whole ideas. This alphabet was simpler to learn and more adaptable, which made it easier to spread. Phoenician merchants carried their alphabet throughout the Mediterranean, and it influenced the Greek alphabet, which in turn influenced the Latin alphabet, the basis of many modern languages today. This spread of writing allowed for better record-keeping, storytelling, and sharing of scientific and philosophical ideas, making it one of the most impactful "inventions" spread across the Mediterranean.

Science and mathematics also traveled across the sea, especially between the Greeks, Egyptians, and later the Romans. In Egypt, knowledge of mathematics was important for building structures like the pyramids and managing the Nile River's floods. When Greek thinkers like Pythagoras and Euclid visited Egypt, they studied Egyptian knowledge and combined it with their own observations to make advances in geometry and mathematics. Greek knowledge then traveled to Rome, where it influenced Roman engineering and architecture. The Romans, in turn, improved upon Greek ideas and developed new technologies, such as aqueducts to carry water to their cities. These ideas and techniques in science, mathematics, and engineering were shared and improved upon, ultimately benefiting all the civilizations connected by the Mediterranean.

The Mediterranean was also a place where different medical knowledge and practices were shared. In Egypt, doctors had discovered ways to treat wounds, perform basic surgeries, and even diagnose some diseases. Greek doctors, such as Hippocrates, known as the "Father of Medicine," learned from Egyptian practices and developed their own medical ideas. Hippocrates wrote down his theories and observations, creating a foundation for Western medicine. His ideas about observing patients, keeping records, and trying to understand the causes of diseases influenced not only Greece but also Rome and eventually the entire Western world. The spread of medical knowledge improved health and care across the region, setting the stage for the future of medicine.

Religious beliefs traveled as freely across the Mediterranean as trade goods did. Long before the spread of major religions, the Mediterranean was full of gods and goddesses that people worshiped, often connected to nature, like the sun, sea, and harvest. As people encountered different cultures, they sometimes adopted or adapted gods and myths. For example, the Greek god Zeus and the Roman god Jupiter share many characteristics because the Romans adopted much of Greek religion. Later, when Christianity emerged in the eastern Mediterranean, it spread quickly across the sea. This new religion traveled through the Roman Empire's vast network of roads and ports, and it reached people from all walks of life. Similarly, Judaism spread around the Mediterranean, with Jewish communities forming in major cities like Alexandria, Rome, and Athens, where they contributed to local culture and ideas.

Even legends and myths spread across the Mediterranean, giving people shared stories and heroes. The epic tales of Homer, like *The Iliad* and *The Odyssey*, told of legendary Greek heroes and were shared far beyond Greece. These stories captured people's imaginations and were passed down for generations, even influencing Roman literature and mythology. The tales of heroes like Odysseus, who journeyed through the Mediterranean, resonated with other cultures, and soon, many people around the Mediterranean were telling similar stories of bravery, gods, and monsters. These shared stories helped create a sense of connection among the different people living around the sea, as they all celebrated the values of courage, honor, and adventure.

Art and architecture were also greatly influenced by the Mediterranean's role in spreading ideas. Each culture had its own style of art, but as they came into contact with each other, artists were inspired to try new techniques and styles. The Greeks, for example, developed their own style of sculpture, which focused on idealized human forms. When the Romans came into contact with Greek art, they were deeply inspired and began creating their own sculptures in a similar style, which spread throughout the Roman Empire. Egyptian art, with its distinct look and use of symbolism, also influenced Greek and later Roman art. Similarly, architectural ideas, like the use of columns, were shared and adapted. Greek columns inspired Roman architecture, and elements of these styles can still be seen in buildings around the Mediterranean today.

The spread of ideas through the Mediterranean also included advances in law and government. The Romans, influenced by Greek ideas, developed a complex system of laws that became the basis for legal systems in many parts of Europe and beyond. Roman law was written down and organized in a way that made it easier for people to understand and follow, and these principles spread throughout the empire. Even today, many modern legal systems trace their roots back to Roman law, thanks to the influence that spread through the Mediterranean.

The Mediterranean, by connecting distant lands and diverse people, created a melting pot of ideas. It was a place where civilizations could interact, learn from each other, and innovate. As each culture contributed something unique, the Mediterranean became not just a sea bordered by different countries but a shared world of knowledge, culture, and history. The ideas that were exchanged across its waters shaped not only the civilizations of the time but also the entire course of history, leading to many of the ideas, inventions, and institutions we have today. Through trade, exploration, and cultural exchange, the Mediterranean's role in spreading ideas has left a legacy that continues to shape the world, proving that this sea was truly a bridge between cultures and a cradle of civilization.

Chapter 16: The Battle for Control of the Mediterranean Sea

The Mediterranean Sea has always been a place of great importance, and because of that, it has also been the scene of many fierce battles as empires and nations fought for control over its waters and coasts. The reason so many different groups wanted to rule the Mediterranean was simple—it was the key to power, wealth, and influence. Whoever controlled the sea could control trade, collect taxes from ships passing through, and expand their territory. They could bring in exotic goods from distant lands and build connections with faraway kingdoms. The Mediterranean was like a giant highway connecting three continents: Europe, Asia, and Africa. Over the centuries, some of the most powerful empires and kingdoms clashed over it, each wanting to rule its precious waves.

One of the earliest groups to try and control the Mediterranean were the ancient Egyptians. The Egyptians didn't try to conquer other lands through the sea, but they built strong fleets to defend their coasts and trade routes. They knew that the Mediterranean was an important source of wealth, allowing them to trade their valuable grain, gold, and papyrus with other countries. However, the Egyptians were soon challenged by the Phoenicians, an extraordinary seafaring people who became one of the first groups to explore and trade all across the Mediterranean. They set up colonies and trading posts in places as far away as Spain and North Africa, establishing a network that allowed them to control much of the Mediterranean's trade. Their ships sailed from city to city, bringing with them goods, ideas, and new ways of doing things. For a while, it seemed like the Phoenicians were unstoppable.

But the Phoenicians' dominance of the sea did not go unchallenged. The Greeks, who were also skilled sailors, started expanding their influence across the Mediterranean. They established colonies in southern Italy, Turkey, and the coastlines of North Africa. As the Greeks built their cities and ports, they clashed with the Phoenicians, especially around important trade routes. The competition grew fierce as each side tried to gain more power and wealth. Greek ships patrolled the sea, defending their colonies and attempting to block Phoenician ships. This was one of the first times that control of the Mediterranean led to outright conflict. The Greeks and Phoenicians would compete over trade, resources, and alliances with local tribes. It was a constant struggle to see who could be the dominant force in the sea.

However, perhaps one of the most famous and long-lasting battles for the Mediterranean happened between two massive empires: Rome and Carthage. Carthage was originally a Phoenician colony, but over time, it grew into a powerful city-state in North Africa, with a mighty navy and a huge empire. Carthage controlled much of the trade in the western Mediterranean, and its ships were feared by others. Meanwhile, Rome, a rising power in Italy, started to see Carthage as a threat. They knew that if they wanted to expand their own power, they would have to deal with Carthage. What followed was a series of brutal wars known as the Punic Wars.

The Punic Wars were some of the largest battles the Mediterranean had ever seen. Rome and Carthage clashed again and again, both on land and at sea, in a desperate fight to control the region. One of the most famous Carthaginian generals, Hannibal, led his army across the Alps into Italy in a daring attempt to surprise Rome. Although he won many battles on land, he couldn't secure the control of the Mediterranean Sea, which remained crucial for the war effort. The Romans, meanwhile, were determined to build up their navy to match Carthage's. They trained their soldiers to fight on ships and developed new tactics, such as the corvus, a boarding device that allowed Roman soldiers to board enemy ships more easily. In the end, Rome's persistence paid off. They defeated Carthage and went on to destroy the city, taking full control of the Mediterranean. This victory gave Rome immense power, marking the beginning of what historians call "Mare Nostrum," or "Our Sea," as the Romans liked to refer to the Mediterranean.

With Rome in control, the Mediterranean entered a period of relative peace and stability under Roman rule. Rome built strong fleets to patrol the sea and protect trade routes from pirates and invaders. This peace, known as the Pax Romana, allowed trade and communication to flourish across the Mediterranean. But even as Rome grew powerful, it faced new threats. Germanic tribes from Europe, nomadic groups from Asia, and later, the powerful Persian Empire from the East all challenged Roman control. While Rome was able to defend its hold on the Mediterranean for a long time, eventually, the empire weakened, and new groups began to fight over its territories.

One of these new powers was the Byzantine Empire, the eastern half of the Roman Empire that survived after the fall of Rome in the West. The Byzantines worked hard to control the Mediterranean because they understood its importance for their economy and security. They fought wars with various groups, including the Vandals, a powerful tribe that had taken over parts of North Africa and disrupted trade in the Mediterranean. The Byzantine navy used advanced ships and tactics to try and maintain control, but it was a constant struggle. Even as they managed to reclaim some lost territories, new threats emerged.

Around the same time, the rise of Islam in the 7th century brought another powerful force into the struggle for the Mediterranean. Muslim armies from the Arabian Peninsula quickly expanded and took control of vast territories, including parts of North Africa, the Middle East, and even parts of Europe. They built a powerful navy and began to challenge Byzantine dominance in the Mediterranean. Battles erupted as both sides sought control, leading to centuries of warfare, trade agreements, and tense standoffs. During this time, the Mediterranean became a battleground between Christian and Muslim powers, with each side trying to gain more influence and secure trade routes. This clash not only affected the politics of the region but also its culture, as ideas and knowledge spread between the Christian and Muslim worlds.

In the Middle Ages, the Mediterranean was still a valuable prize, and new powers entered the struggle. The Italian city-states of Venice and Genoa became wealthy and powerful by controlling trade routes in the Mediterranean. They built impressive fleets of ships and fortified their ports, becoming rivals and occasionally going to war with each other. Venice, in particular, grew rich by trading with both Christian and Muslim lands, bringing in goods from Asia and selling them in Europe. These city-states weren't large empires, but they were influential because they controlled vital parts of the Mediterranean trade network. They used their wealth to fund armies and build even bigger fleets, maintaining control over their territories through cunning alliances and fierce battles at sea.

Meanwhile, pirates became a major problem for Mediterranean trade. Bands of pirates roamed the sea, attacking merchant ships and coastal towns, taking prisoners, and demanding ransom. Some pirates worked for powerful rulers, while others were independent. The Barbary pirates, based along the North African coast, were especially feared. They captured ships and enslaved sailors, causing constant trouble for European nations. To protect their trade and citizens, countries like Spain, France, and Italy invested in large fleets to hunt down pirates and secure the sea.

As time passed, the Ottoman Empire rose to power in the eastern Mediterranean, challenging both the Byzantines and the Europeans. The Ottomans, a powerful Muslim empire, expanded into Europe and the Middle East, capturing Constantinople and turning it into Istanbul. With their large navy and skilled sailors, the Ottomans became a dominant force, controlling much of the eastern Mediterranean. They fought many battles with European powers, including the famous Battle of Lepanto in 1571, where a coalition of European states defeated the Ottoman navy. This battle was a turning point, showing that European powers could stand up to the Ottomans and keep their hold on parts of the Mediterranean.

As European powers grew stronger, they built bigger, more advanced ships and explored new trade routes outside the Mediterranean. Spain and Portugal started exploring the Atlantic Ocean, discovering new lands in the Americas and finding sea routes to Asia. These discoveries shifted some of the focus away from the Mediterranean, as European nations now had access to goods and wealth from other parts of the world. However, the Mediterranean still remained important, especially for countries bordering it.

In the centuries that followed, control of the Mediterranean continued to be a strategic goal for many empires. Napoleon Bonaparte of France, for example, sought to control Egypt and the eastern Mediterranean in his quest to expand French power. Later, during the two World Wars, the Mediterranean was once again a critical battleground. Nations fought to control its waters for military and strategic purposes. Naval battles, submarine warfare, and the protection of supply routes made the Mediterranean a vital area during these global conflicts.

Through all these battles, the Mediterranean proved to be a place where cultures met, clashed, and learned from each other. Although control of the sea changed hands many times, each civilization that ruled its waters contributed something unique to the history of the region. The Mediterranean's story is one of competition and cooperation, showing how a single sea could unite and divide people in their quest for power and influence.

Chapter 17: The Trade Routes that Shaped Ancient Empires

The Mediterranean Sea was the center of one of the greatest networks of trade routes in the ancient world. These routes connected people from far-off lands, allowing them to exchange goods, share ideas, and learn from each other. Each time a merchant set sail or traveled along a dusty road, they brought with them precious goods, fascinating stories, and sometimes even new inventions or ways of thinking. Over time, these trade routes helped shape powerful empires, bringing them wealth and influence, but they also brought challenges as different groups competed for control of the most important paths and ports.

One of the most famous trade routes in ancient times was the route of the Phoenicians. This group of skilled sailors and merchants from the eastern Mediterranean built a powerful network that stretched all the way from their homeland—what is now modern-day Lebanon—across the Mediterranean Sea and into the Atlantic Ocean. The Phoenicians were expert shipbuilders, and they sailed their sturdy ships to places as far west as Spain and as far south as North Africa. Along the way, they set up colonies and trading posts, creating a network that allowed them to exchange valuable goods like cedarwood, purple dye, glass, and metal tools. They traded with nearly every society around the Mediterranean and spread their knowledge of navigation, which other civilizations quickly adopted. The Phoenicians even traded as far as Britain to gather tin, an essential metal used to make bronze, and their influence was so widespread that they helped lay the foundations of trade across the Mediterranean.

Another important trade route was controlled by the Egyptians. Egypt, with its wealth of resources like gold, papyrus, and grain, was highly attractive to other civilizations. Egyptian merchants sailed along the Nile River to reach the Mediterranean, where they exchanged their goods with other cultures. The Nile was the heart of Egyptian civilization, so its connection to the Mediterranean Sea turned Egypt into a key trading power. Egyptian traders exchanged gold, which was especially prized by other civilizations, for materials like copper, wood, and gemstones from places as far away as Afghanistan and Greece. Through their trade, the Egyptians not only gained wealth but also collected ideas, artistic styles, and new technologies that helped their civilization flourish. Egypt's influence extended far beyond its borders, and even the mighty Pharaohs encouraged and supported trade expeditions.

To the east, the Silk Road began to take shape, stretching from China all the way to the Mediterranean. While the Silk Road is often remembered for its overland routes, there was also a "maritime Silk Road" that crossed the Indian Ocean and eventually connected with the Mediterranean. This network of trade routes allowed precious items like silk, spices, gemstones, and exotic animals to travel thousands of miles from Asia to the Mediterranean. Silk, for example, was a prized material that rulers and nobles in the Roman Empire loved to wear because of its smooth texture and beautiful shine. The Roman Empire was one of the biggest consumers of goods from the East, and the flow of trade between Asia and the Mediterranean enriched both sides. While the Silk Road was an expensive and dangerous route to travel, it allowed cultures separated by great distances to share ideas, inventions, and even religions. For example, Buddhism and other spiritual practices spread along the Silk Road, eventually reaching the Mediterranean region.

The Greeks also created a network of trade routes that helped their empire grow. Greek traders sailed all around the Mediterranean, establishing colonies and trading posts in Italy, Turkey, Egypt, and beyond. Each of these colonies became a little piece of Greece in foreign lands, spreading Greek culture, language, and ideas far and wide. The Greeks traded wine, olive oil, and pottery, which were highly sought-after goods throughout the Mediterranean. In exchange, they received goods like grain from Egypt, silver from Spain, and spices from distant lands. Greek traders and scholars brought back new ideas and knowledge, such as advancements in mathematics and medicine, that would shape Greek civilization and make it one of the most influential in history.

The Romans, when they rose to power, took control of many of these ancient trade routes and made them even more extensive. Rome built roads that connected its empire from Europe to the Middle East and down into North Africa, and these roads became important pathways for trade. Roman merchants used these routes to transport goods, while Roman soldiers protected them, ensuring that trade could flourish across the empire. The Romans traded olive oil, wine, and pottery across the Mediterranean and brought back luxury goods like silk from China, spices from India, and ivory from Africa. Roman coins, which were used all over the empire, became a symbol of Roman power and influence. These trade routes brought incredible wealth into Rome and allowed its citizens to enjoy goods from across the world.

In North Africa, the Carthaginians developed their own network of trade routes, which they used to build a powerful empire. Carthage, located in modern-day Tunisia, became a wealthy and powerful city due to its strategic location. The Carthaginians traded with nearly every civilization along the Mediterranean, exchanging goods like metals, textiles, and precious stones. They were also known for trading with African tribes south of the Sahara, bringing back valuable resources like gold and ivory. Carthaginian ships were a common sight on the Mediterranean, and Carthage's wealth helped it grow into one of the most impressive cities of the ancient world.

One unique thing about these ancient trade routes is how they helped spread not just goods but also ideas, art, and culture. When traders from different places met at ports or along routes, they didn't just exchange goods—they shared stories, learned about each other's traditions, and brought new ideas back home. For example, Greek art and architecture influenced the Romans, while the knowledge of mathematics from the Middle East and Egypt eventually reached Europe. Philosophies, religions, and scientific ideas traveled from one civilization to another, enriching the knowledge of each culture along the way. The spread of ideas was one of the greatest impacts of these trade routes, and it helped shape the civilizations that ruled the Mediterranean.

Trade routes also created competition. As different civilizations wanted to control these valuable paths, conflicts and wars often broke out. The Punic Wars between Rome and Carthage were a famous example of how important control of trade routes was. Each side wanted to dominate the Mediterranean's sea lanes and the wealth they provided. Carthage's strong navy and wealth from trade made it a powerful rival to Rome, and the two sides fought fiercely over control of the western Mediterranean. After a series of brutal battles, Rome eventually emerged victorious, destroying Carthage and establishing itself as the dominant power in the Mediterranean.

Pirates were another challenge for ancient trade routes. Bands of pirates would attack ships, seize goods, and take prisoners to sell as slaves. This made trading risky, but it also encouraged ancient empires to build strong navies to protect their merchants. Rome, for instance, sent out fleets to clear the Mediterranean of pirates, ensuring that trade could flow smoothly and merchants could travel safely. Piracy was a constant threat, but it also led to stronger naval forces and alliances between different states that wanted to protect their trade.

The movement of people and goods along these ancient trade routes laid the foundations for the world as we know it today. Without these routes, many important ideas, inventions, and cultural practices would never have spread. Ancient trade connected civilizations and brought about a level of globalization that allowed people to enjoy goods from distant lands, understand foreign cultures, and learn from each other. The Mediterranean Sea was the heart of these ancient trade routes, and it became a place where different worlds met, exchanged, and grew. The influence of these routes can still be seen in the rich cultures and history of the Mediterranean region today.

Ultimately, the trade routes of the ancient Mediterranean were not just lines on a map; they were lifelines for the civilizations they connected. They fueled the rise of empires, inspired explorers, and brought countless discoveries to the world. Each civilization that controlled these routes left its mark on history, proving that the power of trade is more than just wealth—it's the sharing of human culture and the spreading of ideas that shape the world in countless, lasting ways.

Chapter 18: The Rise of the Ottoman Empire

The rise of the Ottoman Empire in the Mediterranean was one of the most significant events in world history, reshaping the balance of power in the region and influencing many aspects of culture, trade, and religion. The Ottoman Empire began as a small state in the late 1200s, but over the centuries, it expanded into one of the most powerful empires of its time. Its growth was marked by military strength, strategic alliances, and clever diplomacy, allowing it to dominate much of southeastern Europe, western Asia, and North Africa, including crucial parts of the Mediterranean coast. This expansion changed the Mediterranean world, bringing new laws, customs, and technologies and leaving an impact that can still be seen today.

The story of the Ottoman Empire begins with the Turkic people who migrated from Central Asia to Anatolia (modern-day Turkey). Among them was a tribe led by a man named Osman, who is considered the founder of the Ottoman dynasty. Osman established a small kingdom in the northwestern part of Anatolia, close to the weakened Byzantine Empire. Over time, his successors—called the Ottomans after Osman—gradually expanded their territory by seizing Byzantine lands and taking advantage of political divisions in the region. The Ottomans were skilled at building alliances with local leaders and using both diplomacy and force to achieve their goals. By forming these alliances, they won support from people within conquered territories, making it easier for them to expand their influence.

One of the key events in the rise of the Ottoman Empire was the capture of Constantinople in 1453. Constantinople, now called Istanbul, was one of the most important cities in the world at that time, serving as the capital of the Byzantine Empire and a major center of trade and culture. It was located on the Bosporus Strait, a vital waterway that connected the Mediterranean Sea to the Black Sea. By controlling Constantinople, the Ottomans could control trade routes between Europe and Asia. Led by Sultan Mehmed II, often called "Mehmed the Conqueror," the Ottomans laid siege to the city, using advanced cannons and military tactics. After several weeks, they broke through the city walls, marking the end of the Byzantine Empire and the beginning of a new era under Ottoman rule. With Constantinople as their capital, the Ottomans were positioned to extend their power across the Mediterranean.

After taking Constantinople, the Ottoman Empire continued to expand into Europe, the Middle East, and North Africa. Under a series of strong rulers, the Ottomans developed a powerful navy that allowed them to control much of the Mediterranean Sea. They built shipyards and fleets, trained sailors and captains, and constructed forts along the coast to protect their territories. This powerful navy was crucial in fighting off rival powers, such as the Spanish and Portuguese, who also sought to control Mediterranean trade. The Ottoman navy clashed with European navies in many important battles, and for a long time, the Ottomans were the dominant naval force in the Mediterranean. Control of the sea meant control of trade, and trade brought wealth, making the empire even stronger.

One of the most famous Ottoman rulers, Sultan Suleiman the Magnificent, played a major role in expanding the empire's reach. Suleiman ruled during the 1500s, a period often called the "Golden Age" of the Ottoman Empire because of its economic prosperity, cultural achievements, and military strength. Suleiman extended Ottoman control over Hungary, the Balkans, and parts of the Middle East, and his navy fought successfully in the Mediterranean, ensuring Ottoman dominance in the region. Suleiman was not only a powerful leader but also a patron of the arts, literature, and architecture, commissioning beautiful mosques, palaces, and gardens that still stand in Turkey and other parts of the former Ottoman Empire. His reign was a time of creativity and wealth, making the empire an attractive place for traders, artists, and scholars from all over the world.

Trade was a central part of the Ottoman Empire's success in the Mediterranean. The Ottomans controlled many of the important ports and cities along the coast, which allowed them to regulate the flow of goods such as spices, silk, and precious metals. Merchants from Europe, Asia, and Africa came to Ottoman-controlled cities to buy and sell goods, bringing with them their customs, foods, and ideas. This made cities like Istanbul vibrant cultural centers where people from many different backgrounds interacted. The Ottomans created a unique system that allowed merchants from different religious and ethnic groups to live and work together peacefully. They respected the beliefs of Christians and Jews, allowing them to worship freely as long as they paid a special tax. This tolerance attracted people from many lands, enriching the Ottoman Empire's culture and economy.

In addition to trade, the Ottoman Empire's influence in the Mediterranean extended to religion and law. The Ottomans were Muslims, and they brought Islamic beliefs and traditions to the areas they conquered. Although they allowed religious diversity, Islam played an important role in the empire's government and daily life. Islamic scholars were respected and often consulted on matters of law and education. The Ottomans developed a legal system based on Islamic law, known as Sharia, but they also incorporated local laws and customs. This combination allowed them to rule over a vast and diverse population without creating too much tension. Their system of government, which was highly organized and efficient, became a model for other empires, influencing governance in the region for centuries.

One of the biggest challenges to Ottoman dominance in the Mediterranean was the growing power of European countries, especially Spain and Portugal. These nations had powerful navies and were looking to expand their own empires. The Ottomans found themselves in competition with these European powers, particularly in the western Mediterranean. This led to several naval battles, with the most famous being the Battle of Lepanto in 1571. In this battle, a coalition of European forces defeated the Ottoman navy, marking the first significant loss for the Ottomans in the Mediterranean. Although the defeat at Lepanto did not end Ottoman control of the eastern Mediterranean, it showed that European powers were becoming stronger and more willing to challenge Ottoman dominance.

Despite this setback, the Ottoman Empire continued to thrive for centuries, adapting to changes in the Mediterranean and expanding into new territories when possible. The Ottomans remained a significant force in the Mediterranean until the 1800s, when political changes in Europe and technological advancements began to weaken their control. By this time, European countries had developed stronger economies, new technologies, and more powerful navies, allowing them to surpass the Ottomans in military and economic strength. The Ottoman Empire began to lose territories, and by the early 20th century, it had shrunk significantly, eventually dissolving after World War I.

The rise of the Ottoman Empire in the Mediterranean had a lasting impact on the region. They introduced a rich blend of cultures, languages, and traditions that are still evident in Mediterranean countries today. Ottoman architecture, such as grand mosques and palaces, still stands in cities across the former empire, showing the beauty and strength of Ottoman design. The Ottomans' unique approach to governing a diverse population influenced later empires, and their emphasis on trade helped to create a network of merchants and markets that connected Europe, Asia, and Africa. Even though the empire has long since disappeared, its influence remains a key part of Mediterranean history.

Through their control of the Mediterranean, the Ottomans also affected European exploration. As European nations sought new trade routes to bypass Ottoman-controlled lands, they explored new territories, leading to the discovery of the Americas and the establishment of trade routes around Africa. In this way, the Ottomans indirectly contributed to the Age of Exploration, which changed the world forever. The empire's dominance in the Mediterranean pushed European powers to find creative solutions, leading to technological advancements in navigation, shipbuilding, and mapmaking.

In the end, the rise of the Ottoman Empire in the Mediterranean is a story of ambition, resilience, and adaptability. The Ottomans built one of the most successful empires in history, shaping the Mediterranean world and influencing countless lives. They ruled through a blend of strength and tolerance, creating a unique society that valued trade, cultural diversity, and learning. Their legacy can be seen not only in the Mediterranean but across the world, where the stories of their achievements, battles, and contributions continue to capture the imagination of historians, travelers, and learners alike. The Ottoman Empire remains a remarkable chapter in the history of the Mediterranean, a testament to the power of vision and determination in building a lasting legacy.

Chapter 19: Mediterranean Islands: Settlements and Legends

The Mediterranean Sea is home to many islands, each with its own history, culture, and legends. Some islands are small, others are large, but all of them have played important roles in the story of the Mediterranean. These islands have served as homes for ancient settlers, safe harbors for sailors, and bases for powerful empires. They have been both points of connection between different cultures and places of mystery and legend. From ancient times to today, Mediterranean islands have captured imaginations with tales of mythical creatures, fierce battles, hidden treasures, and heroic journeys. Each island has its own unique story to tell, and together, they paint a picture of the rich and diverse history of the Mediterranean.

One of the largest and most famous Mediterranean islands is Crete, located south of mainland Greece. Crete was home to one of the earliest civilizations in Europe, the Minoans, who flourished around 3,000 years ago. The Minoans were skilled sailors, farmers, and artists, and they built beautiful palaces with advanced designs, like the famous Palace of Knossos. Legend has it that Knossos was the home of King Minos and that a terrifying creature called the Minotaur, half-man and half-bull, lived in a labyrinth beneath the palace. According to Greek mythology, the hero Theseus came to Crete to defeat the Minotaur and free the people from the monster's terror. The story of the Minotaur and the labyrinth became one of the most famous myths in Greek culture, and it all took place on this mysterious island. Crete's mix of real history and captivating legends makes it a place that continues to fascinate people worldwide.

Another legendary island is Cyprus, located east of Greece and south of Turkey. Cyprus has been settled by different cultures for thousands of years due to its strategic location in the Mediterranean.

The island is famous for its connection to Aphrodite, the Greek goddess of love and beauty. According to myth, Aphrodite was born from the sea foam near the coast of Cyprus, and she emerged from the waters as the most beautiful of all the gods. Because of this, Cyprus became known as the "Island of Aphrodite," and it attracted worshipers who built temples in her honor. Over time, Cyprus was ruled by many empires, including the Egyptians, Greeks, and Romans, each leaving behind their own traditions and artifacts. Today, you can still find ancient ruins on the island that show the incredible mix of cultures that once called Cyprus home.

Sicily, the largest island in the Mediterranean, has a history filled with legends and power struggles. Located at the "toe" of Italy's "boot," Sicily was an important trading hub and a battleground for empires like the Greeks, Carthaginians, and Romans. In ancient times, Sicily was believed to be the home of the Cyclopes, one-eyed giants who worked for the god Hephaestus in his fiery workshop beneath Mount Etna, an active volcano on the island. One of the most famous Cyclopes in Greek mythology is Polyphemus, a giant who trapped the hero Odysseus and his men in a cave during their journey home from the Trojan War. Odysseus cleverly blinded Polyphemus to escape, making this one of the most thrilling tales in Homer's *Odyssey*. Sicily's landscape, with its rugged mountains and powerful volcano, helped fuel these dramatic stories of gods, monsters, and brave heroes.

The island of Sardinia, located west of Italy, is known for its unique ancient culture and mysterious stone towers called *nuraghes*. These stone structures were built thousands of years ago by the Nuragic people, who were skilled builders and farmers. The nuraghes are scattered across the island, and while historians still debate their exact purpose, it's thought that they served as fortresses, meeting places, or perhaps even homes. Sardinia's history also includes legends of giants, and some people believe that the tall stones used to build the nuraghes were created by a race of giants who once lived on the island. These legends, along with the island's unique traditions and language, make Sardinia a fascinating and mysterious part of the Mediterranean world.

Another enchanting island is Malta, a small island south of Sicily that has played an important role in Mediterranean history. Malta's location made it a valuable base for controlling sea routes, and it has been ruled by various empires, including the Phoenicians, Romans, Arabs, and the powerful Knights of St. John, a medieval order of knights who defended the island against invasions. The Knights of St. John built impressive fortifications and protected Malta during the Great Siege of 1565 when the Ottoman Empire tried to take the island. The knights held off the Ottomans, making Malta a symbol of Christian resistance. Besides its heroic history, Malta is also home to ancient temples that are older than the pyramids in Egypt. These megalithic temples, with their massive stones and mysterious carvings, hint at an ancient civilization that valued art and spirituality. Malta's blend of historical significance and ancient wonders has made it a treasure trove for archaeologists and a place of wonder for visitors.

Corsica, an island north of Sardinia, has a rugged beauty that has inspired myths and legends for centuries. Known as the birthplace of Napoleon Bonaparte, Corsica has a unique identity influenced by both France and Italy. It's a place of high mountains, deep forests, and beautiful coastlines, which have helped shape the culture of the Corsican people. Corsica has also been linked to the legend of the hero Ulysses. In Greek mythology, it is said that Ulysses encountered fierce inhabitants on the island during his travels. Corsica's wild, untouched landscape gives it an air of mystery, as if ancient heroes and mythical creatures might still roam its shores.

The Balearic Islands, which include Majorca, Menorca, and Ibiza, are located off the eastern coast of Spain. These islands were settled by different groups over the centuries, including the Phoenicians and Romans. The Balearics became known for their skilled slingers, warriors who could hurl stones with great accuracy and were highly valued as soldiers. Ibiza, in particular, has a rich mix of cultural influences and is known for its ancient Carthaginian roots. According to legend, the god of dance and music, Bes, was worshiped on Ibiza, giving the island a reputation for its vibrant spirit—a reputation it still holds today as a center for music and celebrations. The Balearics' unique combination of history, myth, and celebration makes them a special part of Mediterranean heritage.

Rhodes, located near Turkey, is another island famous for both its history and mythology. In ancient times, Rhodes was home to one of the Seven Wonders of the World, the Colossus of Rhodes, a giant statue of the sun god Helios that stood at the island's harbor. The statue was built to celebrate a victory over an invading force, and it symbolized the strength and unity of the people of Rhodes. Although the Colossus was destroyed by an earthquake, the story of this giant statue lives on as a reminder of the island's ancient glory. Rhodes was also known as a center of learning and trade, attracting philosophers, artists, and sailors from all over the Mediterranean.

The island of Delos in the Aegean Sea is small but holds great importance in Greek mythology. According to legend, Delos was the birthplace of Apollo, the god of the sun, and his twin sister, Artemis, the goddess of the moon. Ancient Greeks considered Delos to be a sacred place, and it became a major religious and cultural center. Temples, statues, and treasures dedicated to Apollo and Artemis were built on the island, drawing pilgrims from all over Greece. Delos was even declared a "free island," where people from different city-states could gather peacefully for worship and festivals. Although Delos is now uninhabited, its ruins and myths remain, reminding us of the island's once-great significance.

Each Mediterranean island has its own personality, shaped by its history, natural landscape, and the myths that surround it. These islands were not just homes for ancient settlers and empires—they were places of wonder and mystery, inspiring tales that have lasted for thousands of years. Whether it's the Minoans of Crete, the Knights of Malta, or the temple builders of Sardinia, the people who lived on these islands left their mark on Mediterranean history and culture. They built monuments, created art, and told stories that captured the essence of their world.

Today, the Mediterranean islands continue to fascinate people from around the world. Visitors come to see the ancient ruins, experience the vibrant cultures, and listen to the legends that make each island unique. The Mediterranean islands are like time capsules, preserving the memories of ancient civilizations and inviting us to imagine the world as it once was. In these islands, past and present meet, creating a magical blend of history and myth that continues to inspire dreams of adventure and discovery.

Chapter 20: Exploring the Mediterranean Today

Exploring the Mediterranean today is like stepping back in time while still being surrounded by the buzz and beauty of the modern world. The Mediterranean Sea, with its vast stretches of blue water and coastlines that touch Europe, Africa, and Asia, is a place where ancient wonders meet today's adventures. People from all over the world come to explore its ancient ruins, swim in its crystal-clear waters, and walk through cities where people have lived for thousands of years. Each Mediterranean country and island offers something unique, and every place has a story just waiting to be discovered.

One of the most exciting parts of exploring the Mediterranean today is visiting the historic ruins and monuments that tell the story of ancient empires. In Greece, the ruins of the Parthenon in Athens still stand proudly atop the Acropolis, offering breathtaking views and reminding visitors of the powerful city-state that once ruled much of the ancient world. Walking among the columns of the Parthenon feels like entering a world of philosophers, warriors, and gods. Nearby in Delphi, travelers can visit the site where the ancient oracle gave mysterious advice to Greek leaders. The whole area is surrounded by mountains, giving it an otherworldly feel that many people find magical.

Italy is another destination that is rich in ancient history. In Rome, the Colosseum stands as a reminder of the grandeur of the Roman Empire. This massive amphitheater, once filled with gladiators, roaring crowds, and fierce animals, now welcomes tourists who are eager to learn about the empire that ruled the Mediterranean for centuries. The Roman Forum, just steps away from the Colosseum, was the heart of ancient Rome, where political discussions, markets, and celebrations took place. Walking through these ruins, you can almost imagine the bustling life of ancient Romans who gathered there.

Not far from Rome, visitors can explore the remains of Pompeii, a Roman city that was buried under volcanic ash when Mount Vesuvius erupted in AD 79. The volcanic ash preserved Pompeii so well that visitors today can still see the streets, buildings, and even some of the artwork on the walls. It's like stepping into a time capsule that shows what life was like for everyday Romans nearly 2,000 years ago. The people who come to Pompeii find it both fascinating and haunting—a reminder of the power of nature and the way time can stand still in the most unexpected ways.

The Mediterranean is also known for its spectacular natural beauty. With its sandy beaches, rocky cliffs, and hidden coves, it offers some of the most stunning coastal scenery in the world. In places like the Amalfi Coast in Italy, visitors are treated to views of steep cliffs that plunge into the blue sea below, with colorful towns clinging to the hillsides. The sunsets over the Mediterranean are unforgettable, with the sky turning shades of pink, orange, and purple as the sun dips below the horizon. For people who love the sea, there are countless beaches to relax on, from the famous beaches of the French Riviera to the hidden gems on the islands of Greece and Croatia.

Speaking of islands, the Mediterranean is dotted with beautiful islands, each with its own personality. In Greece, the island of Santorini is famous for its white-washed buildings and blue-domed churches, which overlook the sea from high up on the cliffs. Santorini is a volcanic island, and the views of the caldera, a large volcanic crater, are breathtaking. People come to Santorini not only to relax but also to see the island's unique landscape and experience its charming villages and delicious cuisine. Mykonos, another Greek island, is known for its lively atmosphere and beautiful beaches, where people enjoy swimming, sunbathing, and exploring the island's charming streets filled with shops and restaurants.

Over in Spain, the Balearic Islands, which include Ibiza, Majorca, and Menorca, are popular destinations for both relaxation and adventure. Ibiza is famous for its nightlife, attracting visitors from around the world who come to dance and enjoy the island's music festivals. But Ibiza also has a quieter side, with beautiful beaches and a peaceful countryside that's perfect for hiking. Majorca, the largest of the Balearic Islands, offers stunning beaches, historic towns, and mountains where people can hike or cycle. The island's capital, Palma, is known for its impressive cathedral and beautiful old town with narrow streets and lively plazas.

In the northwestern Mediterranean, France's Côte d'Azur, or the French Riviera, is another famous destination. The Riviera is known for its glamorous cities like Nice, Cannes, and Saint-Tropez, where visitors can enjoy beautiful beaches, luxury shopping, and delicious French cuisine. The area is also known for its art, as famous artists like Picasso and Matisse were inspired by the region's beauty. The combination of art, food, and seaside relaxation makes the French Riviera a dream destination for many travelers.

On the southern side of the Mediterranean, Egypt offers incredible historical sites along with the beauty of the Nile River. In Cairo, the Great Pyramids of Giza and the Sphinx stand as wonders of the ancient world, attracting millions of visitors every year. Travelers can explore the Nile River, which has been called the lifeblood of Egypt, by taking a cruise that allows them to see temples, tombs, and ancient villages along the river's edge. In Alexandria, a port city founded by Alexander the Great, visitors can experience a blend of ancient history and modern Egyptian culture.

Further west, the Moroccan cities of Casablanca, Tangier, and Marrakech offer a taste of North African culture with Mediterranean flair. Tangier, located at the northern tip of Morocco, has been a gateway between Europe and Africa for centuries. This city, with its mix of Moroccan, French, and Spanish influences, has long been a favorite spot for writers, artists, and travelers. The bustling markets, known as souks, are filled with colorful spices, textiles, and traditional crafts, giving visitors a chance to experience the vibrant culture of Morocco. The Mediterranean coast of Morocco offers beautiful beaches and a warm climate, making it a perfect spot for relaxation.

Across the Mediterranean in Turkey, the city of Istanbul straddles both Europe and Asia, making it a unique destination where two continents meet. Istanbul is famous for its grand mosques, historic palaces, and bustling bazaars. The Hagia Sophia, once a church, then a mosque, and now a museum, is one of Istanbul's most famous landmarks, with its impressive dome and beautiful mosaics. The Bosporus Strait, which connects the Mediterranean to the Black Sea, runs through Istanbul and offers boat tours with stunning views of the city's skyline. Istanbul's mix of ancient history, modern energy, and cultural richness makes it a fascinating place to visit.

One of the most special aspects of exploring the Mediterranean today is the chance to experience the region's cuisine, which is both delicious and diverse. Each country has its own traditional dishes, many of which are made with fresh ingredients like olive oil, vegetables, seafood, and herbs. In Greece, people enjoy dishes like moussaka, a layered casserole with eggplant and meat, and souvlaki, grilled meat served with pita and tzatziki sauce. Italian food is world-famous, and visitors to Italy can enjoy pasta, pizza, and seafood dishes, along with gelato for dessert. In Spain, people love tapas, small dishes that are perfect for sharing, and paella, a flavorful rice dish often made with seafood. North African cuisine brings spices like cumin, coriander, and saffron to the table, with dishes like tagine, a slow-cooked stew, and couscous, a type of grain that's often served with vegetables and meat.

Exploring the Mediterranean today is not only about seeing beautiful places but also about connecting with the history, art, and culture that have shaped the region over thousands of years. It's about wandering through ancient ruins, swimming in clear blue waters, tasting traditional dishes, and meeting people who keep the traditions and stories of the Mediterranean alive. The Mediterranean is a place where visitors can feel the echoes of the past while enjoying the vibrant life of the present, making it one of the most special and fascinating regions in the world to explore.

Epilogue

As our journey across the Mediterranean comes to a close, let's take one last look at the incredible stories this sea has to tell. From ancient kingdoms to legendary heroes, from fearless explorers to brilliant inventors, the Mediterranean has shaped—and been shaped by—the people who lived along its shores. It's a place where cultures met, ideas were exchanged, and history was made.

Today, the Mediterranean is still alive with adventure and discovery. You can visit the ruins of Carthage, sail past the rocky cliffs of Greece, or stand in the shadow of Egypt's pyramids. Every corner of this sea holds traces of the past, reminding us of the empires that once rose and fell, and of the people who dreamed of new horizons.

But the Mediterranean's story isn't finished. The same sea that carried ancient ships now connects modern countries and diverse cultures. Its waters still bring people together, inspiring curiosity, creativity, and exploration. As you step away from these stories, remember that history isn't just something we read about—it's something we continue to shape, just as the Mediterranean's waves continue to shape its shores.

So, whether you dream of becoming an explorer, a storyteller, or a world traveler, the spirit of the Mediterranean is with you. There will always be new places to explore, new stories to uncover, and new wonders to discover. The Mediterranean's legacy lives on in each of us, reminding us that we're all part of the world's grand adventure.

The End.

Milton Keynes UK
Ingram Content Group UK Ltd.
UKHW030822181124
451360UK00001B/226